UNDERSTANDING
EDWARD P. JONES

UNDERSTANDING CONTEMPORARY AMERICAN LITERATURE

Matthew J. Bruccoli, Founding Editor

Linda Wagner-Martin, Series Editor

Volumes on

Edward Albee | Sherman Alexie | Nelson Algren | Paul Auster
Nicholson Baker | John Barth | Donald Barthelme | The Beats
Thomas Berger | The Black Mountain Poets | Robert Bly | T. C. Boyle
Truman Capote | Raymond Carver | Michael Chabon | Fred Chappell
Chicano Literature | Contemporary American Drama
Contemporary American Horror Fiction
Contemporary American Literary Theory
Contemporary American Science Fiction, 1926–1970
Contemporary American Science Fiction, 1970–2000
Contemporary Chicana Literature | Robert Coover | Philip K. Dick
James Dickey | E. L. Doctorow | Rita Dove | Don DeLillo
Dave Eggers | Louise Erdrich | John Gardner | George Garrett | Tim Gautreaux
William Gibson | John Hawkes | Joseph Heller | Lillian Hellman | Beth Henley
James Leo Herlihy | David Henry Hwang | John Irving | Randall Jarrell
Charles Johnson | Diane Johnson | Edward P. Jones | Adrienne Kennedy
William Kennedy | Jack Kerouac | Jamaica Kincaid | Etheridge Knight
Tony Kushner | Ursula K. Le Guin | Jonathan Letham | Denise Levertov
Bernard Malamud | David Mamet | Bobbie Ann Mason | Colum McCann
Cormac McCarthy | Jill McCorkle | Carson McCullers | W. S. Merwin
Arthur Miller | Steven Millhauser | Lorrie Moore | Toni Morrison's Fiction
Vladimir Nabokov | Gloria Naylor | Joyce Carol Oates | Tim O'Brien
Flannery O'Connor | Cynthia Ozick | Suzan-Lori Parks | Walker Percy
Katherine Anne Porter | Richard Powers | Reynolds Price | Annie Proulx
Thomas Pynchon | Theodore Roethke | Philip Roth | Richard Russo | May Sarton
Hubert Selby, Jr. | Mary Lee Settle | Sam Shepard | Neil Simon | Isaac Bashevis Singer
Jane Smiley | Gary Snyder | William Stafford | Robert Stone | Anne Tyler
Gerald Vizenor | Kurt Vonnegut | David Foster Wallace | Robert Penn Warren
James Welch | Eudora Welty | Colson Whitehead | Tennessee Williams
August Wilson | Charles Wright

UNDERSTANDING

EDWARD P. JONES

James W. Coleman

The University of South Carolina Press

Published by the University of South Carolina Press
Columbia, South Carolina 29208
www.sc.edu/uscpress

Manufactured in the United States of America

25 24 23 22 21 20 19 18 17 16
10 9 8 7 6 5 4 3 2 1

Library of Congress Cataloging-in-Publication Data
can be found at http://catalog.loc.gov/.

ISBN 978-1-61117-644-5 (cloth)
ISBN 978-1-61117-645-2 (ebook)

This book was printed on recycled paper with
30 percent postconsumer waste content.

For a third time to my sons,
Jay and Lee Coleman,
whose love continues to support me

CONTENTS

SERIES EDITOR'S PREFACE

The Understanding Contemporary American Literature series was founded by the estimable Matthew J. Bruccoli (1931–2008), who envisioned these volumes as guides or companions for students as well as good nonacademic readers, a legacy that will continue as new volumes are developed to fill in gaps among the nearly one hundred series volumes published to date and to embrace a host of new writers only now making their marks on our literature.

As Professor Bruccoli explained in his preface to the volumes he edited, because much influential contemporary literature makes special demands, "the word understanding in the titles was chosen deliberately. Many willing readers lack an adequate understanding of how contemporary literature works; that is, of what the author is attempting to express and the means by which it is conveyed." Aimed at fostering this understanding of good literature and good writers, the criticism and analysis in the series provide instruction in how to read certain contemporary writers—explicating their material, language, structures, themes, and perspectives— and facilitate a more profitable experience of the works under discussion.

In the twenty-first century Professor Bruccoli's prescience gives us an avenue to publish expert critiques of significant contemporary American writing. The series continues to map the literary landscape and to provide both instruction and enjoyment. Future volumes will seek to introduce new voices alongside canonized favorites, to chronicle the changing literature of our times, and to remain, as Professor Bruccoli conceived, contemporary in the best sense of the word.

Linda Wagner-Martin, Series Editor

CHAPTER 1

Understanding Edward P. Jones

Several lines of Langston Hughes's poem "Mother to Son" could be Edward P. Jones's mother's words to him describing her life and partly foreshadowing his: "Well, son, I'll tell you: / Life for me ain't been no crystal stair. / It's had tacks in it, / And splinters, / And boards torn up, / And places with no carpet on the floor— / Bare." The fact that Jones's family "moved 18 times in 18 years" (Murphy 23) as his mother struggled to keep herself and her three children together sums up much of their "no crystal stair" life. Perhaps because of this reality, Jones is a truly humble, down-to-earth man, but also because of his relationship to his mother and his own too often precarious life, he ironically has risen to greatness as a writer.

Born in Arlington, Virginia, on October 5, 1950, Jones, a bachelor who has always lived alone and does not own a car, still resides in a rented apartment in Arlington, and has lived mostly in this area around Washington, D.C., except for time away earning his BA (1972) at College of the Holy Cross in Worcester, Massachusetts, and his MFA (1981) at the University of Virginia. Jones's father left when he was a preschooler, and his mother Jeanette, an impoverished, illiterate maid and menial worker, took care of him, his sister, and his brother and influenced him greatly. Jones went to public schools in Washington, D.C. Always having a love for reading, he read comic books early in life; he did not begin to read novels until he was thirteen. When he began reading black writers, the novel that made the greatest impression on him was Richard Wright's *Native Son*. He wrote his first fiction as a sophomore at Holy Cross, but did not consider writing as a career while in college. When he graduated in 1972, the highlight was his mother's attendance after she had had several strokes: "He didn't expect his mother to be able to make the trip. 'When I walked into the stadium, I looked up in the stands, and there she was,' he says. 'They told me later that when they were driving here, and she got her first glimpse of Holy Cross up on the hill [overlooking Worcester], she started crying. That was the first time she'd ever seen it'" (Murphy 25).

When he returned to Washington after graduation, his mother became ill and died in January 1975. After she died, Jones, working sporadically and barely able to take care of himself, published his first story in *Essence* in 1976. The four hundred dollars *Essence* paid him allowed him to stay in Washington instead of moving to New York with his sister as he had planned. Later, he went to graduate school in creative writing at the University of Virginia. After he returned to Washington, he worked as a columnist and proofreader for *Tax Notes,* a tax-related newsletter in Arlington, from 1983 to 2001. This was a steady job although not a high-paying one, and during this time he published *Lost in the City* (1992), his first collection of stories and first major work, influenced by James Joyce's *Dubliners* and Richard Wright's *Uncle Tom's Children. Lost in the City* was nominated for the National Book Award (1992) and won the PEN/Hemingway Award (1993). This did not mean the end of Jones's hardship, though. In 2001 he lost his job; however, ironically this also freed up his time to work on his novel about slavery, *The Known World* (2003). While writing the novel, he was depressed and on and off medication; his imagination of the misery of the slaves in the novel turned out to be therapy for his own pain. The novel has become the foundation of his fame. Among several prestigious awards, it won the Pulitzer Prize and earned Jones the McArthur "Genius Award" in 2004. (The "Genius Award" is a $625,000 grant awarded annually by the McArthur Foundation, usually to twenty to twenty-five people in different fields who have done exceptional work and show exceptional potential.) His second collection of stories, *All Aunt Hagar's Children* (2006), was nominated for the PEN/Faulkner Award.

Both of the short story volumes set in Washington and the novel set in Virginia before the Civil War connect emotionally and culturally to Jones life in the area, and to the larger contemporary cultural milieu of black and white America. Jones has said about the emotional and cultural influences on *All Aunt Hagar's Children:* "I have spent . . . all my life in D.C. Ninety percent of what I remember and use in this work has to do with my mother and the other ten percent comes from the people I knew when I was growing up who were adults born and raised in the South. They brought all that they knew and what they did and what they learned in the South to Washington" (Graham 432). This could also apply to *Lost in the City.* Further, Jones has said that in America he still sees definite signs of the institution of slavery that he portrays in *The Known World:* "It is as if slavery were legal now." All Americans "absorb and become part [of slavery's legacy that] is in the culture" (Graham 427, 428).

Jones has been teaching at George Washington University in Washington, D.C., since 2010. Some recent interview statements indicate that while teaching he is waiting for his next writing project to take shape in his imagination, as happened over the years with *The Known World*. However, Jones's literary achievements already place him in the canon of contemporary American literature. Biographies of Jones are readily available, including through online sources, and he gives accounts of his life in many printed and online interviews. (Much of the account of his life here comes from *Encyclopedia of World Biography* and interviews by Michelle Murphy, Sarah Anne Johnson, Marita Golden, and Mary Emma Graham.)

The Known World thematically and structurally constitutes a symbol of African American experience that stands for *everything*, a *historical whole*, a *totality*. On at least two occasions, in an anonymous interview appended to the Amistad edition of *The Known World* (4) and in an interview by Sarah Anne Johnson ("The Image You Woke Up With" 89), Jones says that he is the "god" of his work and clearly implies a godlike literary vision. Using his godlike literary vision that is frequently both proleptic (sees the future) and analeptic (sees the past), Jones tries to depict and, through the overall structure of the writing, tries to *symbolize* everything, a historical whole, a totality of African American experience.

The same thematic and structural approach is central to *The Known World*. As the novel's disjointed, incongruous chapter titles suggest (chapter 1, "Liaison. The Warmth of Family. Stormy Weather," for example), Jones integrates disparate, fragmentary narrative and thematic elements and innumerable characterizations into the loosely connected central story; this integration of structure, theme, characterization, and story symbolizes the totality of experience. This totality is everything, a historical whole that often relies on prolepsis and analepsis to bring it together. It is a "unity of place [that] . . . allows for the re-membering of lost time; it permits artistic resurrection" (Berman 236) of everything. (The narrative vision and the overall approach in the short stories are generally similar to the novel.)

The novel is sometimes difficult to understand, but one thing that makes it easier as well as delightful is humor, often based on irony. Part of the humor comes from the narrative voice revealing the absurdity of oppression that is so much a part of the historical black experience. At times, listening to the narrator is like listening to good jokes and anecdotes that ironically expose the underlying reality of the absurd. The narrator is funny because the reader knows that he is telling the truth. (The short stories are sometimes similarly humorous.)

The story told in *The Known World* consists of multiple, fragmented, unlimited stories, and at the same time is an all-in-one story of the totality of the black experience: a central story about Henry Townsend's plantation, many stories about life in the era of slavery, many stories about the future and past in which the narrator reveals proleptic and analeptic vision, and after the last chapter, a concluding story of a godlike view that sees everything. In the central narrative, black, slave-owning Henry dies near the beginning, but his wife, Caldonia, takes over the plantation. In another story that is a fragment to the central story but still related to it, white slave patrollers, although they know he is free, sell Henry's father Augustus into slavery in Georgia, where his new owner, Hillard Uster, murders him, and Sheriff John Skiffington kills Henry's free mother, Mildred, when she tries to protect the Townsend plantation's black slave overseer Moses after he has run away from slavery. There are many other stories about people and situations on the Townsend plantation and elsewhere that are more peripheral to the central story than Augustus and Mildred's, and almost countless anecdotes and accounts of the future and past. In all of this, pervasive humor directed at the morally corrupted characters and the oppression of slavery generally creates an ironic vision that is highly critical.

The second of the three parts of the title of chapter 5, "A Cow Borrows a Life from a Cat," is an example of narrative fragmentation and critical humor. It refers to an episode that centers on a dispute between two of the white slave patrollers, Harvey Travis and Clarence Wilford, whom Manchester County pays eight dollars per month (155). The dispute occurs because Travis sells Wilford a dry cow that he claims gives plentiful milk, "though in fact more milk fell from the sky than came from the cow." The cow was "something Joseph might have dreamed up and warned Pharaoh about" (158). Travis's attempted scam notwithstanding, the cow miraculously starts giving milk after Wilford buys her. Wilford's wife, Beth Ann, "took one teat and aimed it at a cat standing to her side. The cat closed its eyes and opened its mouth and drank. Its tail had been in the air, but as it drank, the tail lowered and lowered until it was at last resting on the ground" (156). "The cow swung its tail and chewed its cud. It farted." Sheriff Skiffington resolves the dispute by convincing Travis, who agrees reluctantly, to stop trying to get his fifteen dollars for the cow back in exchange for Wilford letting him get milk twice a week, but only if he stops harassing Wilford. In the context of the episode's title, somehow, someway, for some strange reason, the cow "borrows" life from the cat, apparently as indicated in the movement of their tails, even after the cow has miraculously found a new milk-producing life, even when the cow seems to nourish the cat. On one hand, this is a fragmented story disconnected from the other stories, one which stands on its own through its fortuitous ironic humor that resides in the nonsensical, surprising, and unexpected. On the other, it is ironic and humorous that Wilford cannot see that his deception and depravity coincide with his life as a slave patroller who hunted down, brutalized, and sometimes killed human beings, and it is ironic and laughable that the highly Christian sheriff only seeks justice in a dispute between white men and does not see the injustice of slavery. This emphasizes the immorality and lack of vision of white people living with moral certainty and supporting the institution of slavery, which was so obviously wrong. The southern slave culture did not see this, but the novel's vision encompassing the totality of African American experience sees this and much more.

The concluding pages after the last chapter call the vision godlike, implying a thematic critique and the creation of the totality of black experience in *The Known World*. In the conclusion, there are two artworks created by the character-artist Alice. One is literally a structural replica of life: "*There are no people . . . just all the houses and barns and roads and cemeteries and wells in our Manchester* [County, Virginia]. *It is what God sees when he looks down on Manchester*" (384). The other art piece is a structural replica, too, but it includes the people. Calvin Newman says: "*It is your* [his sister Caldonia's] *plantation, and again, it is what God sees when He looks down. There is nothing missing, not a cabin, not a barn, not a chicken, not a horse. Not a single person is missing. I suspect that if I were to count the blades of grass, the number would be correct as it was once when the creator of this work knew that world*" (385). Although it may not be discernible from the normal, usual human perspective, everything is where it should be structurally and working out for the good from this perspective. The perspective is godlike, but it is also the creation of the ex-slave artist Alice, who now has a larger view, which is like the view of *The Known World*. Alice's words regarding her life seem to carry a moral critique of slavery that affirms the positive: "*I have been good as God keeps me*" (386).

Besides describing the godlike view, Calvin points out the well-being of the escaped slaves now living in Washington that suggests a future much greater and bigger than slavery. It is significant that Calvin dates his letter April 12, 1861, the date of the start of the Civil War that led to this future and that is part of the ongoing totality of African American experience. In this hypothetical time, God keeps Alice as she and the other characters flourish: "*All that is here is owned by Alice, Priscilla* [an ex-slave] *and all the people who work here, many of them, to be sure, runaways. . . . Jamie* [Priscilla's son] *comes and goes as a student in a school for colored children. He is as fine a young man as any father or mother could want.*" Even back in the "real" time of slavery, the novel presents a sense of continuity, transcendence, and survival that is emblematic of an ongoing totality larger than any oppressive present. *The Known World* ends: "Her meals to Moses [who had his Achilles tendon cut by slave catcher Oden Peoples for trying to escape] would be until the end. [The slave] Celeste was never to close down her days, even after Moses died, without thinking aloud at least once to everyone and yet to no one in particular, 'I wonder if Moses done ate yet'" (388).

There are broad and general structural and thematic connections between the novel and short story collections and among all three works. Structurally in the novel, narrative and thematic elements and characterizations coalesce with the central story through the figures of the pieces of art at the conclusion. If not before, then at least at the end the reader can understand the idea of a totality of African American experience that Jones wants to capture symbolically.

The arrangement of stories in *Lost in the City* is part of a general symbolism in Jones's work, which the last story highlights. The volume starts with the youngest character, five-year-old Betsy Ann Morgan in "The Girl Who raised Pigeons," and progresses to the oldest, eighty-six-year-old Marie Delaveaux Wilson, in the fourteenth and last story, "Marie." The progression from the experiences of the youngest to the oldest symbolizes the totality of black life, which Marie at the end "hears" when she listens to tapes of her own history.

Both the female and male main characters in the fourteen stories are "lost in the city," imperiled in their Washington, D.C., environment in one way or another, but they are not always, and perhaps never, imperiled and "lost" beyond hope. This is mainly true because of the thematic context created by all of the stories. The progression of stories creates an overall context, in which there are intimations of connections to the South and its black tradition of strength and survival, and there is psychological and literal movement back and forth between the South and the North that puts the characters in touch with the tradition that allows them to survive or makes survival a possibility. The character who may be the most "lost" is Lydia Walsh in "Lost in the City," the eighth story. Lydia seems to have absolutely no sense of a positive direction to move in and no sense of anything that can save her. Her characterization is ironic because she has a law degree from Yale and is making a lot of money. However, Lydia is not necessarily more "lost" than the high-school-aged girls in "The Night Rhonda Ferguson Was Killed," the third story; Caesar Matthews in "Young Lions," the fourth story; Joyce Moses in "His Mother's House," the seventh story; or Vivian L. Slater in "Gospel," the eleventh story. The chances for psychological or physical survival for the other characters seem better, Woodrow L. Cunningham in "A New Man," the twelfth story, being an example, and Marie in the last story being the best example. However, in the overall context, there is for the characters in each story, including Lydia, at least the intimation of the saving connection, the potential pathway back and forth between the South and North, which makes survival a possibility.

The idea of a totality of black experience comes together in "Marie." Listening to her account of her life on tapes, Marie hears a story with black historical relevance which she was unaware of telling, a story about her parents' naive but still sustaining faith and hope while living in the South, and about her own naive youthful striving that nevertheless led her safely to Washington. This history shows that the oppression black people underwent forged in them and their descendants the positive vision of hope and faith that allowed them to transcend this same oppression. This history on the tapes is the totality of experience that connects black people, now "lost in the city"; the history is the potential saving pathway, back and forth, between the South and the North.

The short-story collections are connected volumes that also coalesce to represent a totality of black experience. There is no clear central story in the two volumes as there is in the novel. However, in "Tapestry," at the end of *All Aunt Hagar's Children,* tapestries can encompass "one hundred, two hundred, three hundred," "maybe even a thousand" years (377), again representing the totality of black experience.

Although *All Aunt Hagar's Children* is similar in many ways to *Lost in the City,* the arrangement of stories is different, and the general thematic emphasis and direction of the stories are somewhat different. In *All Aunt Hagar's Children,* usually through a minor character, there is a connection to the correspondingly numbered story in *Lost in the City.* The settings of *All Aunt Hagar's Children*'s stories are sometimes earlier, sometimes later; this means there is not the same progression from the youngest character in the first story to the oldest in the last. However, the collective experience of all the characters, particularly with the stories' connections to the stories in *Lost in the City,* still represents a totality of black experience, and individual stories portray the same totality. Throughout the volume almost all the characters live imperiled lives in Washington, initially at least, and the psychological pathway between the South and the North that can sustain and save black people is just as important as in the first volume. The characters in *All Aunt Hagar's Children,* though, are generally more successful in finding the pathway that connects and sustains. This is true for eighteen-year-old Anne Perry in "Tapestry," the last story, but it is also true for most of the other characters. The fates of characters at the end of a few stories are perhaps more ambiguous and more troubling, for example Laverne Shepherd in "The Devil Swims Across the Anacostia," the tenth story, and Horace Perkins in "A Rich Man," the twelfth story, but in no story is a character as "lost" as Lydia in "Lost in the City."

However, the biggest difference in the second volume is its predominant focus on characters that are artist figures and the theme of artistry. This focus is most explicit in "All Aunt Hagar's Children," the fifth story; "A Poor Guatemalan Dreams of Downtown Peru," the sixth story; "Root Worker," the seventh story; and "Tapestry," the fourteenth story. "Old Boys, Old Girls," the fourth story; "Common Law," the eighth story; and "Blindsided," "A Rich Man," and "Bad Neighbors," the eleventh, twelfth, and thirteenth stories, respectively, are the ones in which the portrayal of artists and artistry is not apparent. Nonetheless, looking at the context of all the stories in the collection, the reader arguably finds the role of the artist and the theme of artistry implied, although not explicit, in all the other stories. At the end, "Tapestry" confirms the primary focus on artists and artistry through its portrayal of Anne Perry, the tapestry maker. Because they sometimes portray artists and their artistic devices, approaches, and techniques and sometimes reveal the complex workings of artistry, the stories often have a quality that is more dreamlike, imaginary, and supernatural, and are more experimental and much longer, making the volume itself more difficult than the earlier collection.

CHAPTER 2

Meaning, Structure, and Story in *The Known World*

Edward P. Jones's Pulitzer Prize–winning novel *The Known World* (2003) starts with a focus on the end of a fifteen-hour day for Moses, a slave and the black overseer for a black slave owner named Henry Townsend; it is the day in the summer of 1855 that Henry dies. After the day is over, Moses goes into the woods, undresses, lies on the ground naked, and masturbates, which we learn later indicates that he is in touch with and knows the physical landscape of Henry's plantation but, significantly for his immediate future, is totally ignorant ("world stupid" 14–15) about the geographical space beyond it. *The Known World* also ends with an episode that includes Moses 388 pages later, when his life has changed significantly. Although in chapter 5 the novel shows that he was a much more sympathetic human being earlier in his slave life (170–74), Moses now is both a slave *and* a mean, abusive overseer. Once a slave himself, Henry always wanted to be more beneficent than other masters (chapter 3, 64) and turns out not to be as brutal as some white masters, but he still does perpetrate at least one atrocious act on a slave after he tries to escape (chapter 3, 93–96) and exploits black labor just like white masters. The stories of Moses the black overseer and his black master Henry are dominant stories in the narrative, so although white people generally commit more horrific acts against black people, a major part of this novel is about black people abusing, oppressing, and enslaving other black people.

However, one should not think the novel is a justification for the role of white people in slavery or an apology for the institution of slavery itself. In the novel, grounded in the myth of white supremacy (whiteness defined by the myth of having "pure white blood"), white male dominance, and black inferiority (blackness defined by the myth of having "one 'drop' of black blood"), slavery is a hierarchal system of power that, at its bottom line, used the claim of white superiority to oppress black people for white economic gain. Aristocratic white men, the system's primary progenitors and benefactors, have the most power and privilege and uphold the ideas of white supremacy and sanctified white womanhood, particularly sanctified aristocratic white womanhood, in a hierarchy of race, class, and gender. Although they reap very few economic benefits from slavery, because they are still white and enjoy some social and cultural privileges of whiteness, poor white people largely support aristocratic ideas of whiteness and support the system. Poor whites come under white aristocrats in the hierarchy. In the novel at least, Native Americans conspire with all whites to uphold slavery, but occupy a nebulous place somewhere alongside or just below poor whites and free blacks in some cases of free birth and white-looking skin. However, they are definitely above slaves. Very much contingent upon and mediated by the specificity of original free or slave birth status and/or relative lightness and darkness of skin color, free blacks are sometimes higher in the system than Native Americans and definitely higher than slaves, whom they frequently oppose or conspire to oppress. They are, however, still black and racially inferior. Mostly dark-skinned field slaves are at the bottom. Women of all races, classes, and dark or light skin colors (for black women) have their racial, class, and skin privileges and/or liabilities, but are often subject to male privilege attendant to their race and class. This hierarchy may not cover everything in the novel, but it is largely true. Sometimes the system's dynamics (and other details in the novel) are even more complicated and nuanced; in any case, the hierarchy is absolutely horrific, always potentially deadly, especially for those at the bottom who can never securely escape their place.

While its primary goal was aristocratic white men's attainment of power, privilege, and economic gain, slavery pandered to the need of all people to feel superior to and take advantage of others in the hierarchy beneath them. It forced those lower in the hierarchy to internalize negative traits and attitudes that go along with feelings of inferiority, or to act in other ways that were negative. (Henry, a black man who saw nothing wrong with opportunistically seizing the power of a slave owner, is the primary example of a negative response by someone low in the hierarchy). Slavery morally and psychologically corrupted all people, men and women; too often, people of all races and classes nefariously maneuvered within slavery's hierarchy of power or otherwise internalized or acted out its nefarious influence. However, the novel's dominant theme is the triumph of black people over slavery and oppression, and since it shows that at least one racist poor white man named Barnum Kinsey, a slave patroller, can surprisingly think and act morally toward black people (chapter

6, 214; chapter 9, 301–4), perhaps it points to the hope that all people can evolve toward the transcendence of racism that is the legacy of slavery.

Between the beginning and the end that also includes Moses, acting in a role similar to the role Jones has defined for himself as writer, the omniscient narrator tells a story with an unlimited view like a god[1] who sees and knows all but tells, shows, and specifies what it chooses, and within individual chapters and throughout the novel, the narrative evokes this godlike view that critiques and criticizes slavery and ultimately projects the novel's dominant theme. Godlike, the narrative jumps back and forth in the past, present, and future, and deals with the stories of Moses and Henry, many other major and minor characters, and a plethora of peripheral characters. The present time of the novel's central plot(s) is about two months beginning in July 1855, but the story ranges back far in the past and looks into the future from the late nineteenth to the late twentieth century. Jones uses his godlike literary vision to depict and, through the fragmented, episodic structure of the narrative, symbolizes a historical whole, a totality of African American experience.

An engaging irony directing attention to close scrutiny and sometimes an inseparable sarcasm, both often producing a wry, humorous, and/or odd "flavor," are two of the godlike omniscient narrator's major tools to create a context to critique slavery. Irony does not always adhere to a strict dictionary definition: words sometimes have underlying meanings that are not obvious on the surface; characters are missing the underlying meaning of what they are saying or doing; or readers find out something that is the opposite of what they first thought. Irony can also reside in a somewhat unexpected perception or understanding: the revelation we see when the narrator with unlimited vision sometimes chooses to make comparisons and connections among people, scenes, and situations in the past, present, and future that we would likely never make. The narrator makes many surprising revelations, not all of which compare and connect in this way, so not all revelations fit this definition. However, many of the revelations do fit the definition and are ironic in this context, and much of the novel is ironic.

As in the other chapters, in chapter 1 the words of the title, "Liaison. The Warmth of Family. Stormy Weather.," suggest the ironic, sarcastic critique. "Liaison" apparently refers to Moses as a link between Henry, his household (including house slaves), and the field slaves who live in cabins beyond the house. "The Warmth of Family" goes back some years in the past, and is about Henry's father Augustus's struggle to buy himself, his wife Mildred, and Henry out of slavery. "Stormy Weather" is about the man who owns Augustus and his family, William Robbins, a brutally inhumane white man and the richest man in Manchester County; he has "storms" in his head, seizure-like occurrences blotting out memory periodically that he perceived "as the price to be paid" for having a black mistress and black children (25). It quickly becomes clear in chapter 1 that, because of slavery, Moses is degraded and depraved, Augustus and his family have to suffer unbelievable hardship as slaves and ex-slaves, and Robbins is an unimaginably bad person. Perhaps the first two parts of the chapter's title might seem to indicate the potential of something good in human relationships or interactions, but it quickly becomes clear that all of the words of the title are ironic and sarcastic.

Throughout the novel, irony, sarcasm, and wry humor about slavery are also evident in short descriptions of incidents and brief quips, such as in chapter 1: "No white person wanted to imagine what would have happened if those five slaves [who were attempting to escape and were caught, brutalized, and murdered] had doubled back, heading south and away from freedom [instead of heading north toward freedom as they were], and got to [a house where three white women were]" (26). Ignoring the illogic of the slaves reversing their course to freedom, white people rely on the ideology of slavery, which dictates that the rape of white women was somehow in the slaves' plan, to justify brutalizing and murdering them. In different ways and instances, the novel's language and overall portrayal employ irony, sarcasm, and wry humor to reveal the unmitigated evil of the system of slavery.

Augustus's ordeal to attain his freedom and to keep his family together, the ironic "warmth of family," portrays the horrible reality of slavery in chapter 1. Augustus, a highly skilled carpenter and a craftsman who keeps part of the money he earns when his owner Robbins hires him out, buys his freedom when he is twenty-two (14), which one can extrapolate to be 1829, works three more years to buy the freedom of his wife, Mildred, in 1832 (15) and an additional eleven years to buy his son Henry's freedom, which does not happen until 1843 (44) in chapter 2. During the whole eleven-year period, Augustus and Mildred go to visit Henry on Sundays, but cannot actually go on Robbins's property because he has ordered Augustus not to come on his land unless he is making a payment on Henry (18). Part of this terrible ordeal is Henry's actions in the intervening years because of his strange indoctrination to become a slave owner. By fall 1834, when he is nine or ten (his age is not specifically clear), through his inattention to his parents, Henry is already revealing his attachment to Robbins, which will lead to him becoming a slave owner in later chapters: "Sometimes Henry did not show up, even if the cold was bearable for a visit of a few minutes," and his parents have to hope that a slave or someone will come by who can go to tell Henry they are there. It is "in mid-February, after they had waited two hours," that Augustus gets angry and pushes Henry to the ground (19). Henry tells Robbins, who punishes Augustus for doing "something to my boy, to my property" by disallowing any visits for a month. Also, because Robbins discovers that Henry is intelligent, he increases his price (17, 28) and thus the time it takes Augustus to buy him.

Throughout the novel, the omniscient narrator speaks in an ironic, sarcastic, humorous voice and demonstrates a godlike vision by tying together in an encompassing pattern all the characters who play important roles (and almost countless others),[2] almost countless episodes[3] complexly structured, and a complex, dizzying chronology. Like the entire novel, chapter 1 develops in episodes separated from each other by breaks in the text. There are eleven separate episodes in the chapter, with settings in 1855, 1855, 1855, 1855, 1855, 1830, 1834, 1840, 1840, 1840, and 1840, respectively. Throughout the chapter are references to the 1860 census (7), to an 1806 act of the Virginia House of Delegates governing freed slaves (15), seemingly to "mid-February" 1835 after the "fall that year, 1834" (18–19), to the 1830 and 1840 censuses (22), to Robbins's feelings about his head "storms" in 1841 (25), and to the 1837 murder and hobbling of slaves attempting to escape (26). These episodes are also mainly or partly about or introduce characters who are significant in addition to those above: a supposedly crazy slave named Alice (whom we first see as she secretly watches Moses masturbate (3–4), and who turns out to be not at all crazy); Henry's wife, Caldonia (as she takes care of him when he approaches death and then dies); Fern Elston, the freeborn black schoolteacher of free black children; the husband and wife field slaves Elias and Celeste; and Robbins's free black children Louis and Dora and their mother, Philomena, Robbins's black mistress whom he buys from another rich white slave owner and then frees (115).

After chapter 4, the episodes in the chapters do not reference different years nearly as much as in chapters 1 through 4, perhaps making the plot easier to follow, but overall the structure and chronology of the novel are complex and dizzying. The fragmented, episodic structure, often nonlinear chronology, and portrayal of multitudinous characters make sense in the context of the novel's godlike vision, symbolizing a historical whole, a totality of African American experience.

Chapter 2, "The Wedding Present. Dinner First, Then Breakfast. Prayers Before an Offering.," carries on the story of Augustus, Mildred, and Henry and introduces other characters who play central roles in the portrayal of slavery. Compared to the eleven in chapter 1, chapter 2 has only six separate episodes set in a more linear timeline, respectively in 1840–41, 1841, 1841, 1843, 1843, and 1843, but as is the case throughout, the omniscient narrator encompasses multiple, sporadic time references. These references are to 1820, 1829, and 1849 (40), to a University of Virginia historian's book in 1979 (43), to 1851 (44), and to Robbins buying slaves for Henry in a period of time before 1850 (50).

The most important new characters the chapter introduces are John Skiffington, who is first the deputy and then becomes sheriff in Manchester County; John's wife, Winifred, whom he meets in 1840 and marries in 1841 (30–31); his cousin Counsel Skiffington from North Carolina, who comes to the wedding; and Minerva, a slave who is ironically the human "wedding present" Counsel and his wife, Belle, give to John and Winifred (31–32). John is a Christian whose religion will not allow him to abide slavery. However, as the novel will show, he has no understanding of the irony of still having the racist thinking that upholds slavery (which is part of the reason he accepts Minerva as a gift in spite of his antislavery feelings) and of being a sheriff who enforces laws that do the same. In spite of being from Philadelphia and having some associations with Quakerism (30), Winifred does nothing to separate or distinguish herself from John. Counsel goes back to North Carolina after the wedding, but circumstances will bring him back later. Unlike John, he totally supports slavery and shows no complexities or contradictions in his thinking. Minerva later becomes John's sexual obsession, although he does not act on his feelings. It is not until near the novel's end (380–82) that we learn that Minerva has a rebellious attitude toward slavery, seemingly sparked by what Belle says to Winifred when she gives her as a gift at the beginning: "She will answer to the name Minnie, but her proper name is Minerva" (32).

John becomes sheriff in 1843 when Robbins pushes out his boss, Sheriff Gilly Patterson; it is the escape of Robbins's slave Rita in 1843 that settles Patterson's fate. Rita escapes with the help of Augustus and Mildred on the day they secure the freedom of Henry (44–50). Rita, who takes care of Henry after Mildred gets her freedom, is so terrified of remaining in slavery after Henry leaves that she vomits up "dinner first, then breakfast" (44–45). Augustus is absolutely terrified at the idea of helping Rita, but he finds the strength to do so. He hides her under a blanket in the wagon and later ships her to New York in a box of canes he has made for an Irish merchant. Surprisingly, Henry, who is nineteen or twenty now (it is not clear which) and has grown close to Robbins, never tells Robbins what happens (44, 49). John also never finds out what happens, but the escape of Rita leads to his becoming sheriff and brings him into the story about slavery.

"Prayers Before an Offering" of the chapter title is an episode (50–53) about Rita's safe arrival in New York. The episode does not seem to relate well to the novel's general story; however, it does relate if one keeps in mind the omniscient narrator's often ironic, godlike vision and what the narrator reveals through it.

A summary of part of the episode and the previous one showing Augustus and Mildred sending Rita away helps show the relationship. Opening the box in New York along with his mother, Mary O'Donnell Conlon, is Timothy, the stepson of the Irish merchant to whom Augustus is sending the box of canes. Timothy is the son of Mary's first husband, who died on her voyage from Ireland to America aboard the HMS *Thames,* the voyage where she met the merchant (50–51). As the German Protestant captain watched, the boy said "ten Lord's Prayers and ten Hail Marys" (51) before his father was buried at sea. He said ten prayers because, from a perspective of oppressive Protestantism in Great Britain, an "Irish prayer was obviously worth only a tenth of what a German [Protestant] Prayer was worth." Also, Mary believes that America has had an effect tantamount to oppression on her family: ". . . America, the land of promise and hope, had reached out across the sea and taken her [first] husband [who died] . . . and America had taken her baby [who also died on the voyage]—two innocent beings in the vastness of a world with all kinds of things that could have been taken first. She held nothing against God. God was simply being God. But she could not forgive America and saw it as the cause of all her misery" (51–52). In the previous episode, as Augustus nails her into the box, Rita and Mildred comfort each other in the faith that God will keep them safe and bring them together in the "bye and bye," where they will not be slaves (48).

Here, the narrator's vision is ironic not just because it is the opposite of what we expect in line with the standard definition of irony; it is also ironic because it brings together people and situations and makes comparisons and connections that are surprisingly odd. The narrator says that Mary survives to be more than seventy-five years old (52), in spite of the cruel deaths of two family members that she blames on America. When Mary opens the box, Rita has survived the cruelty of American slavery and then the almost unimaginable hardship of forty-one hours in the box (50–51). So there is seemingly a comparison and a connection between an Irish and black slave woman's survival of potentially deadly and oppressive experiences related to America. Also, in the portrayals of Rita, Timothy, and Mary, there seemingly are very general comparisons and connections between religious faith and the survival of people who are oppressed. If so, settings and situations are so disparate as to be again odd and surprising. It also seems that the narrator's godlike vision encompassing different experiences reveals something hopeful and uplifting in the potential of human beings to endure and transcend[4] in spite of the horrible pain and suffering they endure, which goes along with the novel's main theme regarding slavery.

Besides the irony in the language of chapter 2's entire title, and the irony in the comparisons and connections made in episodes that correspond to "Dinner First, Then Breakfast" (44–50) and "Prayers Before an Offering," there are also sarcasm and odd, wry humor in the two episodes that are hard to separate from the irony. In the former episode, after Augustus has nailed Rita very tightly in the box and sent her off, with no way for her to get out or move very much on a forty-one-hour train trip, Henry asks, "How she gon do her business?'" (49). Augustus answers, "A little bit at a time." It seems that Henry should not have to ask the question, but then again Augustus's answer seems to solve an obvious problem just as well as any other answer. However, it turns out that "doing her business" "a little bit at a time" does not help Rita. This is because, ignoring the words "THIS SIDE UP WITH EXTREME CARE" that the Manchester County shipping agent has written on the box, someone along the way has turned it over and left Rita lying on her stomach. When she gets to New York and Mary and Timothy open the box, the first thing they see is that Rita has "done her business" all over herself. The story is sarcastically making a point about the utter humiliation and hardship of slavery, but there is wry humor here because the narrator is telling the story with an odd emphasis and attention to detail that make it humorous. The humor accentuates the point about oppression; sarcasm and odd, wry humor contribute to the novel's very effective irony.

Chapter 3, "A Death in the Family. Where God Stands. Ten Thousand Combs.," is the novel's longest chapter; it explores the immediate aftermath of Henry's death at his plantation and in the surrounding community, gives details of the personal histories of Elias and Celeste and of their relationship, introduces Stamford (57), a slave who has a prominent role in the rest of the novel, and starts to go more deeply into the life of Fern Elston, another character with a prominent role. It has eighteen separate episodes: The first five are set in 1855; the sixth begins in 1855 and ends earlier in 1847; and the last twelve are set in 1847. Although it has the most episodes of the twelve chapters, chapter 3 largely adheres to an easy-to-follow timeline first in 1855 and then 1847, with a reference probably to 1825, Elias's "last day with his mother" thirty years before Henry's death (77–78), and to what is probably 1846, when Henry purchased Celeste "a year or so before" he bought Elias sometime in 1847 (79).

The narrator does, however, somewhat complicate the timeline further by looking into the future beyond 1855 to the end of the lives of Elias and Celeste's soon-to-be six-year-old slave daughter Tessie, who will live to be ninety-seven (67), the end of the lives of three-year-old twin slaves Henry and Caldonia, named after the plantation's black master and mistress, who will both die at eighty-eight (68), and the end of the lives of seven- and four-year-old sister and brother slaves Delores and Patrick, who will die at ninety-five and forty-seven, respectively (68–69). The doll Elias is now making for Tessie "would be with her until her last hour," as a very old free woman probably in 1946. Likely in 1938, the twins will die old and free. Caldonia will die before Henry; having "had a good and happy life with a good wife and many offspring with their offspring" (68), Henry will decide to "to up and die" in order to "follow his sister." Delores will die a free woman in old age, probably in 1943. Patrick will die free too, but he will die much younger, probably in 1898, "shot three times by a man as [he] came out of the man's bedroom window after being with the man's wife" (68). Even in the case of Patrick, who dies fairly young and carelessly, obviously the vision of the future that the godlike narrator projects speaks of these children living far beyond slavery. Given their youth now, the children's transcendence of slavery will not be as remarkable as that of some of the older slaves, but still greatly remarkable nevertheless.

Looking ahead in the lives of characters as the narrator does here is not exactly the same thing as in the episodes corresponding to "Dinner First, Then Breakfast" and "Prayers Before an Offering" in chapter 2, but it is similar. In both instances, the narrator makes surprising comparisons that are revelatory and thus ironic in generally the same way.

While not ironic according to my definition of irony in the novel, there are additional surprising revelations that, along with its sarcasm and wry humor, contribute to a generally odd, literarily effective quality. In this context, one kind of revelation is supernatural. In chapter 3, the narrator reveals that two five-year-old slave boys "had been plagued by identical nightmares for weeks. What Grant dreamed one night, Boyd would dream the next. And then, days later . . . Boyd's dream would go across the lane and settle into Grant's dreaming head" (67). Revelations of the supernatural appear throughout the novel. (Earlier in chapter 2, the narrator says that "the slave boy Baker and the two white Otis boys . . . burst spontaneously into flames in front of the dry goods store in 1849" (40). In later chapters, Stamford will have supernatural experiences.)

The main substance of what happens in chapter 3 concerns the reaction to Henry's death, Elias's preoccupation with escaping and attempting to escape when Henry bought him in 1847, and his ensuing marriage to Celeste after his capture. "A Death in the Family" and "Where God Stands" (55–77) refer to the present in 1855 and deal with the reaction to Henry's death. The free community of black people around the plantation mourns Henry; the house slaves seem to be sad, too, but except for Moses none of the field slaves are sad. The title's implied idea that there is a unified family reaction to Henry's death is ironic. After Henry dies, Caldonia tells the gathered slaves that "God stands with us" (64), which she has heard someone else say, and which is obviously ironic because she is talking about God standing with her and with slavery. The chapter starts to provide some in-depth portrayal of Caldonia, whose morality and human depth turn out to be questionable at best.

"Ten Thousand Combs" (77–103) goes back to 1847; it ironically refers to Elias telling Celeste that he will "make [her] a comb for every hair on [her] head" (100). After witnessing the breaking of the gift he has made, a comb that was "certainly one of the crudest and ugliest instruments in the history of the world" (99), he says this in a comical scene when he is courting her before their ensuing marriage. Elias came to Henry's plantation only wanting to escape. He and Celeste did not get along because she thought that, when he saw her, a woman with a crippled foot, he "felt he was watching a show with a cripple woman and . . . enjoyed it" (79). He could not explain his attraction to Celeste: he somehow became interested in her only after he tried to escape, and for punishment Henry paid the Cherokee slave patroller Oden Peoples a dollar to slice off part of his ear. Although they are slaves at the bottom of slavery's hierarchy, Elias and Celeste ironically become two of the novel's most substantive characters, Celeste probably being *the* moral exemplar in the novel. A lot of their moral substance starts to become clear in the chapter in the portrayal of their relationship with Luke, the eleven-year-old slave boy who befriends Elias after his ear slicing, and whom Henry hires out to a man who works him to death (82–88, 96–97, 103).

Fern Elston, the black, freeborn, light-enough-to pass-for-white teacher of free black children, introduced in chapter 1, is also a character with moral and human substance (or who at least develops it) that the narrator starts to talk about more: she changed because something "had shifted with Henry's death, but the greatest shifts were to come very soon, after the gambler Jebediah Dickson [who apparently is a slave too] entered her life" (73). Before Dickson, she did not "mingle with 'any slave that was not house broken.'" After Dickson, "she was never to see the world the same again."

Fern, perhaps primarily, along with Henry and Robbins, are the central characters in chapter 4, which also focuses on Augustus and Mildred; entitled "Curiosities South of the Border. String Tricks in a Doomed City. A Child Departs from the Way. The Education of Henry Townsend.," the chapter has as its central topic Henry's "education" to become a slave owner. It has fourteen separate episodes and perhaps the most complex chronology in the novel. Although the time is not always clear, it seems that the episodes are set respectively as follows: in 1881; sometime between 1841 and 1843; sometime before 1843; in about 1843; in about 1843; in "the early days of the patrollers" (130), probably in 1843; in "the spring and early summer" (133) of Fern's first marriage, an unspecified time in the 1840s and 1850s before 1855; in the same unspecified time before 1855; in 1881; in about 1843; in about 1843; in 1881; in 1855; and in the 1860s sometime during the Civil War. As is often true, the narrator also refers to other disparate times besides the years of the settings of episodes: for example, to the 1994 sale of a pamphlet about blacks owning slaves (106); and to a day "years later" when Robbins's black daughter Dora and white daughter Patience would see each other for the first time (119–20). (The narrator mentions the meeting between daughters again in chapter 12 [363].)

Fern has been the teacher of free black children in Manchester County for years, and the question in chapter 4 is who is the one who "educates" Henry, whom Robbins asks Fern to give a basic education after Augustus buys Henry's freedom from Robbins, right after Henry has become a slave owner by buying a slave, Moses, from Robbins (126–30). Since he is such a rabid supporter of slavery and so strongly antiblack, Robbins's positive feelings and strong support for Henry seem strange, but Robbins is a strange man capable of surprising relationships with black people. This starts with what he feels for his black mistress, Philomena, the mother of Dora and Louis. It is not perhaps love that he feels for Philomena, but he certainly has an almost unbreakable attraction to her, and she certainly has power over him because of this (114–22).

The relationship with Philomena and consequent affection for his black children[5] by her relate directly to Robbins's feeling for and support of Henry. Robbins begins to rely on Henry as a force of stability in his life during the eleven years between the time that Augustus buys his freedom and Henry's, but what makes his reliance on Henry clear to him is the comfort that Henry gives his children when Robbins—in Richmond, having taken Henry with him—assaults Philomena after she runs away with their children (118). (The "String Tricks in a Doomed City" of the chapter's title referring to this incident is another example of irony in the chapter titles. Contrary to what we might expect, the words allude to Henry in Richmond comforting Dora and Louis during the assault by using a "Jacob's Ladder" figure: "Henry had found a piece of string from somewhere and with the string he was making and unmaking Jacob's Ladder" to comfort and calm the children. Similarly, at the very end of the chapter (144–45), we find out that the city of Richmond is "doomed" because the next time Philomena sees it after this (sometime before 1843) is during the Civil War, when it is burning. After this incident in Richmond, Robbins decides that the "world would not be very good to the children he had had with Philomena, but whatever world it would be, he wanted Henry in it for them" (121). This explains much of Robbins's support of Henry—for example, setting him up as a slave owner, selling him land, selling him slaves, and getting Fern to teach him so that he will know the proper relationship between himself and slaves (122–30).

In the chapter, the narrator continues to make surprising revelations and to create a wide range of ironies: Fern teaches Henry at Robbins's request, and Augustus and Mildred unsuccessfully try to teach Henry, whom slavery should have already taught, how evil slavery is, but it is Robbins the white slave owner who really "educates" Henry, the black ex-slave owned by Robbins, to be a slave owner.[6] After he catches him "wrestling with" a "nigger," his first slave whom Robbins sells him (122, 140), Robbins decides to get Fern to teach the black slave owner Henry so that he will know how to deal with his "nigger" slaves. Fern teaches Henry, raising him to literacy, but although she is a slave owner herself, Fern cannot "educate" him to be the kind of slave owner he becomes. The narrator makes this clear by saying that the slaves of Fern and her husband lived closer to their masters than any slaves in Virginia: "Those Elstons didn't have slaves, colored people said, they had neighbors who happened to be slaves" (134). It is unclear when the real "education" specifically takes place. However, it is Robbins who successfully "educates" Henry to become a slave owner with strange reasoning, which is apparently persuasive to Henry because of Robbins's influence over him: "Don't settle for just a house and some land, boy. Take hold of it all. There are white men out there, Henry, who ain't got nothin'. You might as well step in and take what they ain't takin. Why not? God is in his heaven and he don't care most of the time. The trick of life is to know when God does care and do all you need to do behind his back" (140–41). Nothing that Augustus and Mildred can do or say (135–39), including Augustus—in utter outrage and exasperation—hitting him and breaking his shoulder with a cane he has made, can dissuade Henry from being a slave owner (138–39).

Chapter 4 also begins a sequence of focuses on Fern's 1881 interaction with Canadian pamphleteer Anderson Frazier (128–29, 134–35, 141–43), who wrote a series of pamphlets on "curiosities" of the South, the most successful among them being one about Negroes who owned other Negroes. (Chapter 8 also portrays this interaction [245, 250, 260].) The meeting between Fern and Frazier portrays her relationship with Jebediah Dickson, which shows how she becomes one of the novel's most morally substantive characters.

In chapters 5, 6, and 7, the omniscient narrator continues the ironic, sarcastic, humorous critique of slavery; however, although the narrator still sometimes complicates the timeline with sporadic references to the past and future, the primary settings of episodes in these chapters change from focuses on multiple years to a more uniform chronology. These chapters are a transition to a portrayal largely of six weeks to two months after Henry's death in 1855 in chapters 8 through 12, where the novel reaches a denouement, although it does not end.

Its twelve episodes seemingly set entirely in 1844, chapter 5 is "That Business Up in Arlington. A Cow Borrows a Life from a Cat. The Known World."; the most important part of the chapter is probably the section corresponding to "The Known World" (166–77), which obviously repeats the novel's title. Another section that is highly ironic, like most in the novel, this one is about a man in John Skiffington's jail named Jean Broussard, a native Frenchman and now an American citizen. He is the man who sells Moses (who is with a slave named Bessie) to Robbins (166–75) (who in turn sells him to Henry) and is in jail for killing his partner and co-owner of Moses in a drunken brawl (168–69). John has a map in his office, made by a German living in France (174–75), with the legend "The Known World" on it. Broussard tells John that he is from where the map was made and "I can get you better, bigger map" (174). John turns down the offer and, solely because of his French accent (176–77), Manchester County convicts and hangs Broussard for killing his partner. The point here is about slavery's "known world" that the novel portrays. This world first and foremost oppresses black people, but it is also a world in which Broussard's accent gave him "the stench of a dissembler" (177). Jurors would have accepted Broussard's reasons for the murder if he "had sat on the stand and told his whole story without an accent." Broussard is a white male American and a slave owner/seller, but he is not the right kind of "known" American because of his accent. He is not part of the "known world" as the Americans in the slave-owning South know the world.

Chapter 5 further reveals the irony of John Skiffington being a Christian who supports slavery, and portrays Moses as he was before having the supposed power of a black slave overseer corrupted him. On the trip to Winifred's cousin Clara's house to reassure her against her paranoia about the danger of her one slave, and to settle a dispute between two of his slave patrollers, John twice relies on reading his Bible (153–54, 161–62), apparently trying to reassure himself about "God's plan" (161–62). Although a Christian, he has never questioned whether a brutal, oppressive institution like slavery is Christlike and part of God's plan. With regard to Moses, at the time that Robbins bought him, before he became Henry's overseer, he was much more humane; he pleads with Robbins to buy his fellow slave Bessie too because "we together, her and me. . . . Please, master sir, she and me be family" (172).

Set largely in 1855, the second longest chapter (one page longer than chapters 4 and 9), separated into only eight episodes however, chapter 6 has the usual ironical title, the parts of which do not mean what they seem to mean: "A Frozen Cow and a Frozen Dog. A Cabin in the Sky. The Taste of Freedom."; its major developments deal with Stamford and Augustus Townsend. The episode corresponding to "The Taste of Freedom" (209–20), one of the novel's three longest, is about Augustus after he is free, but is not solely about what freedom figuratively "tastes" like to him. It is also about what Augustus's freedom papers literally taste like when the white slave patroller Harvey Travis eats them (212), and then sells the free Augustus back into slavery (212–16). The fate of Augustus afterward is a major part of the rest of the novel.

An incident involving Stamford in the sections portraying "A Cabin in the Sky" (190–209) is central in the later chapters, too, and the life-changing experience that Stamford has in these sections is also significant in the novel's thematic development. When Stamford was twelve, a grown slave told him that he would always need relationships with young women ("young stuff") (57, 190, 197) to survive slavery, and now at forty (57, 71) his pursuit of young women, who no longer want him, is a constant source of friction among the slaves. As a result, Stamford has a fight with another slave over a young woman who has rejected him, and the slave beats Stamford badly (193–94). Stamford's beating leads to Caldonia having Moses come to the house after work daily to give her a report on what has happened, thus preparing the way for another major sequence of events in the remainder of the novel.

The rejection by the woman making it clear that he can no longer get young women, which the ensuing fight confirms, convinces Stamford that slavery is no longer bearable and he needs to die. Trying to fulfill his death wish, he attempts to get killed by lightning by walking recklessly in the woods during a storm. He had always wanted only "a nothing stool way off in the corner of heaven that nobody cared about" (201), but during his experience in the storm he sees "a cabin flying his way through the rainy air" (205–6). This turns out to be a supernatural experience that transforms Stamford into a better person with deeper humanity who can consequently survive slavery, and who can also leave a positive family legacy (206, 353–54). The revelation of his unlikely change under circumstances that are both unlikely and supernatural has a quality of the ironic, and it is ironic that the transformation of Stamford, formerly a profligate, is significant in the thematic outcome of the novel showing slaves successfully coping with slavery. Further, his experience is another example of the narrator's revelation of the supernatural that adds to the odd, literarily effective quality of the novel. Although the chapter is largely set in 1855, there are slight complications in the chronology revealed in Stamford's portrayal. For example, the narrator refers to the time when the forty-year-old Stamford was twelve, apparently 1827, when the man told him he always needed "young stuff" to survive slavery (190); the time when he was "five and it had not been long since his parents had been sold away" (192), apparently 1820; the future time in 1987 when a woman in Richmond designed a street sign in Stamford and his wife's name (206); and again the future time in 1952 when a historian wrote about the floods in the days after Stamford walked out into the storm (207).

The beginning of the chapter (179–90) is about Caldonia Townsend's twin brother, Calvin Newman, and their father, Tilmon (a former slave who purchased his freedom (183), whom his freeborn wife Maude (184) poisons to keep him from selling their slaves (66, 184); Calvin turns out to play an important role, particularly at the novel's end. Because he is gay (188–90), he is a visionary who tries to see a different world than slavery. Ironically, the "frozen dog" of the chapter's title is a dog photographically "frozen" in a picture of New York City life that Calvin has. (The "frozen cow" refers to Tilmon's memory of his youngest brother whom his master sent to find a lost cow in a snowstorm: they found "boy and cow huddled and frozen together" [183].) The dog was "looking off to the right" (189): "There was a whole world off to the right that the photograph had not captured." Calvin's visionary imagination of a different world also implies and is an ironic play on the "known world" of the novel's title and chapter 5's title.[7] Further, the ironic revelation of what the "frozen dog" (and "frozen cow" too) means supplements the novel's rich oddity.

One of the shorter chapters, with only twenty-two pages and six separate episodes, and a largely straightforward chronology set mostly in 1852, "three years before Henry died" (223), chapter 7 is entitled "Job. Mongrels. Parting Shots." It mainly brings Counsel Skiffington and his especially virulent racism, even in a virulently racist society, back into the novel so that he can play a large role in the final chapters. It is impossible to distinguish between dream and reality after smallpox kills everyone but him on his Johnston County, North Carolina, plantation (223–26), and Counsel wanders all the way from North Carolina to Texas (236) in an indeterminate, delirious state of mind. Ironically, throughout the chapter, the evil, racist Counsel, who has made black people suffer so much, has a Job-like feeling about his vicissitudes; "mongrels" refers to Counsel's dreamlike state in which he encounters both dogs in Texas that are literally mongrels (236–37) and people who are figuratively mongrels ("Counsel thought, Texas was being emptied out of filth," 241); and "parting shots" is about him finally in frustration giving his horse two "parting shots" in the head with his pistol when he balks (242–43).

At the beginning of chapter 7 the omniscient narrator gives an ironic revelation (221–23) in the story about the people responsible for bringing smallpox to Counsel's plantation and destroying it. The revelation is that from the beginning Counsel was not, as he thought and as seemed to be true, the slave owner in control of his slaves and his fate; instead, he was subject to much greater and wider forces, as manifested in the dynamics of the lives of a man and woman from Europe and one of his creditors from North Carolina. In talking about the life of the woman, Saskia Wilhelm, the narrator develops the revelation. The woman once worked as a maid for families in New York: "One of those families was the one in the photograph that Calvin Newman owned [chapter 6, 189]. The frozen dog in the picture was named Otto" (222). The narrator shows a confluence of realities that brings together a proponent of slavery, Counsel; an opponent of slavery, Calvin, who envisioned a different world; and

Saskia, the woman coincidentally involved. Saskia had been a maid and then a prostitute (222) but has no direct connection to slavery. However, she does strike against slavery by inadvertently helping to bring about the destruction of Counsel's plantation. The point is not that the narrator's revelatory story "means" anything specifically, but that the narrator portrays a wider reality affecting slavery than is initially apparent that, if anything, points to its demise.

Except for the last episode in chapter 12, and other disparate, sporadic references by the narrator, the setting for episodes in chapters 8 through 12 is entirely in 1855. Chapter 8 begins the novel's move toward the conclusion of its major plot events, which takes place about two months after Henry's death, and its summation after chapter 12. The major characters in the last five chapters—Fern Elston, Moses, Caldonia Townsend, Augustus and Mildred Townsend, Alice, Elias and Celeste, John Skiffington, and Counsel Skiffington—have already established their roles.

Chapter 8's nine episodes are about Fern and her interaction with Jebediah Dickson and the relationship between Moses and Caldonia, which mainly sets the direction of the plot for the remainder of the novel. The strange-sounding name "Scheherazade" that, along with "Namesakes" and "Waiting for the End of the World," is part of the chapter's title is the name of the Persian queen who is the storyteller in *One Thousand and One Nights;* she told stories night after night to the king because her life depended on entertaining him. After Stamford's beating and Caldonia's order that he report to her what happened daily, Moses at first senses that Caldonia wants more than reports of daily events (chapter 6, 208), and then slowly but surely he falls into the pattern of a "Scheherazade" who entertains her with tales about the exploits of her husband and his dead master Henry, as it will ultimately turn out with the purpose of attaining his own freedom and taking Henry's place. Moses starts with modest tales about Henry and then proceeds to much bolder, more elaborate fabrications (261–66). He continues to enthrall Caldonia with stories until he finally seduces her at the chapter's end (273–74), revealing the meaning of the last part of the chapter's title: "He kissed the open hand and his world did not end. She pressed her hand to his face and when he looked up at her, she leaned down and kissed him, and still the world did not end."

The other parts of the chapter show Fern growing to appreciate black humanity through her experience with the escaped slave Jebediah who, in spite of what seems true, insists that he is free and acts like he has the rights of any human being[8] (256–57); Fern's growth as a person who can respect black people, represented by her purchase of Jebediah (254–55) and his manumission (260), is one of the novel's important positive examples. Although everyone in Manchester County knows she is not, the freeborn, slave-owning Fern is light enough to pass for white, which is what the Danville, Virginia (252), owner of the "dark pecan" colored Jebediah (248) thinks when she buys him (255). (In line with the novel's fashion of ironic, odd portrayals, "Namesakes" refers to what Jebediah does after making it to Washington, D.C., following his experience in what he sees as the "demon state" of Virginia (260–61), Fern's positive change notwithstanding: he names his daughter Maribelle, after a horse he had to shoot while he was at Fern's, and names his son Jim ("if he had wanted to name him James, that was what he would have done"), after the horse that brought him to Washington.)

The narrator gives more details about Fern's relationship with Jebediah that leads to her change in chapter 9, but the chapter is more about the journey of Augustus Townsend after his kidnapping, John Skiffington's attempt to find Augustus and see justice done in his case, and Moses's progression in his relationship with Caldonia to the point where he sets up the escape of his wife and son so that he can be with her. Set entirely in 1855 with twelve separate episodes, the chapter continues chapter 8's *relatively* straightforward chronological focus, leading to the conclusion of major plot events. The title, "States of Decay. A Modest Proposal. Why Georgians Are Smarter.," refers to portrayals that we would not expect when reading these words.

"States of Decay" and "Why Georgians Are Smarter" turn out to be the narrator's descriptions of the attempts of Darcy, the slave speculator who buys Augustus (212–15), to sell him and Augustus's attempt to regain his freedom; the language is ironic, and so is the use of the humorous and comic to highlight the horror and tragedy of slavery. When Augustus pretends to be deaf and dumb to prevent himself from being sold in South Carolina, Darcy says: "You done lost your hearin here in South Carolina, that it? Lost your tongue, too, huh? What did you lose in North Carolina? Your Pecker? And Virginia, your brain, what little there is of it? And what it gonna be in Georgia? Your arms? And then your legs in Alabama and Mississippi . . . ?' (278). Darcy tries to get a man in Georgia to buy Augustus by praising Georgians for being smart and giving America its best president. After the man says there has been no president from Georgia, Darcy says: "There ain't? Well, there damn well should have been. And I'll tell you somethin'—there will be a president from Georgia and real soon" (314). Stennis, Darcy's slave lackey who helps him kidnap and sell other black people, says: "There will be five at least, as far as I can tell. Maybe ten. Maybe ten. There'll be ten if I have anything to do bout it. Could go to be twenty or thirty." Darcy had an "unkempt beard that went to his knees and much of his body covered in [beaver] pelts" (213) and only "two teeth in his head" (283). He is as depraved and degenerate as his physical description indicates, and Stennis is just as degenerate and depraved. Augustus, on the other hand, is an exemplar of work and perseverance. He has worked to buy his freedom, worked three more years to buy Mildred's, and about ten more to buy Henry's, and now he is once again "illegally" enslaved and in the power of depraved degenerates. If it were not clear how tragic slavery was, Augustus's situation makes it clear. However, in spite of the insulting, stereotypical allusion to Augustus's brain, both scenes are still humorous; humor ironically emphasizes the tragedy of slavery that traps Augustus and creates depraved degenerates like Darcy and Stennis.

In other episodes in the chapter, John helps further to define his character through his attempts to find Augustus, and reunites with Counsel, who somehow finds his way back to him (281) after chapter 7's experience. Around the times of Augustus's kidnapping and Fern's encounter with Jebediah (286–87, 289–90), which are about the same, Mildred goes to Caldonia and she, Caldonia, and Fern go to John to report Augustus missing (282–83). Having been hired as a deputy by John upon his return (281–82), Counsel and not John is at the office, but Counsel does not tell John about the women's report when he returns. In the meantime, the poor white slave patroller Barnum Kinsey, who is a product of slavery's racism but also somehow heroically above it at the same time, tells John about Augustus's selling/kidnapping because he thinks it was wrong (301–5). John later discovers Counsel's negligence when he goes to Mildred's and she tells him that they did report to Counsel that Augustus was missing. John severely scolds Counsel for dereliction of the law ("you were hired for the law's sake" [309]), which presages what happens between them later.

It is more John's dealings with Harvey Travis and his brother-in-law, the Cherokee Oden Peoples, that informs his characterization, however. In spite of supposedly believing in the rule of law that pertains to free black people as well as slaves (309–10), John only admonishes Harvey and Oden because they sold Augustus: "I don't want to hear anything like this about yall again" (310). He moves to self-justification by asking confusing questions: "Was [Augustus] not doomed by virtue of the color of his skin?" (311). How would the words of a white man who was a "cheat and a brute [Harvey Travis who tried to sell the 'dead-cow']" (154–60) and the words of Oden Peoples, an Indian, which were "worth only half since he was an Indian" (311), weigh against the words of a white "drunkard," Barnum Kinsey? He essentially solves the problem by muddling the whole situation in a self-subterfuge of questions combining racism, class prejudice, and moral judgment, while taking no substantive action against Harvey and Oden. (However, John's self-questioning does reveal how sometimes nuanced dynamics of race and class can confuse slavery's hierarchy.) Because of this, it seems that John is not the uncompromising proponent of the law that he pretends to be. Also, since he "asked for God's guidance" with Augustus's case but "dreamed of Minerva that night," maybe he is not a good Christian, too.

The "modest proposal" of the chapter's title is hardly modest: Moses asks Alice to carry out a plan for her escape and that of his wife, Priscilla, and his son Jamie, so that he can, he fantasizes, marry Caldonia. Even after he started to have sex with Caldonia, still the "sun did not rise very high in Moses' life, and it was only one day at a time and no one day was kin to the next" (286). So his future was still very tentative. However, one day when they make love and she asks if he is "going to come back tomorrow" (292), Moses begins to change. He begins to think that his wife and son "could not live in the same world with him and Caldonia. . . . Where did a slave wife and a slave son fit in with a man who was on his way to being freed and then marrying a free woman? On his way to becoming Mr. Townsend?" (292–93). He begins to make plans for the future—plans with his freedom and marriage to Caldonia in them.

Moses's plans lead to a sequence of events and developments that come together with others in this chapter as the novel moves toward the end. Primarily, after Moses proposes to Alice that she, Priscilla, and Jamie escape, Alice makes it very clear that she is not crazy and carries out the escape (293–98), which leads to John's suspicion and questioning of Moses after he reports the escape to Caldonia (298–301).

Also set entirely in 1855, chapter 10 is slightly more than half the length of chapter 9, although it has one more episode (total thirteen); a fairly clear timeline develops from Tuesday, the day the chapter ends, to "Sunday," the first part of the title of chapter 12, five days later. Entitled "A Plea Before the Honorable Court. Thirsty Ground. Are Mules Really Smarter Than Horses?," the chapter is primarily focused on Moses and Caldonia, Elias and Celeste, and John. Moses runs away after unsuccessfully demanding that Caldonia free him (324–25, 329–35). Before he does, he forces Celeste to work in the fields six-months pregnant and have a miscarriage, making Elias hate him even more than he did because of Moses's earlier mistreatment of him (85–86, 325–28). The great humanity and moral stature of Celeste starts to be evident because she still cares for and tries to take care of Moses in spite of this (331–35). In the meantime, John's world begins to fall apart too because two other slaves from Caldonia's plantation escape three days after Moses, which he knows could motivate Robbins to force him from his job (337–40). The chapter concludes, "That was Tuesday" (340), the day the other two slaves escape.

The development of an often humorous, odd, rich literary quality and the use of engaging, attention-directing, sometimes humorous irony continue in the chapter. Ironically, "A Plea Before the Honorable Court" is Moses's plea before Caldonia to free him while she thinks about a white woman in Bristol, Virginia, beaten for having sex with her slave (292, 301), pleading before the judge: "your honorable court, am I not still white?" (324–25). "Thirsty Ground" alludes to the dry ground ready for Celeste's blood when she miscarries (326). "Are Mules Really Smarter Than Horses" is ironic, too, but its humor is even odder. It refers to Moses, during one of his stories to Caldonia, saying "mules are smarter than horses" (321). It also refers to a conversation between Caldonia's house slave Bennett and John Skiffington. After Bennett reports the escape of the two slaves and John sees that he cannot maneuver a mule and wagon, in exasperation John asks why he does not ride a horse when he cannot handle a mule; Bennett replies, "a horse ain't near as smart as a mule" (339). The words create an odd, wry humor in direct comparison to Moses's earlier words simply because they are basically the same, but the syntax is different. The actions and words of Moses and Bennett create a wry critique of slavery. Maybe humor here does not ironically highlight the horror of slavery through contrast in exactly the same way it does in the scenes with Augustus, Darcy, and Stennis. Still, somewhat similarly, humor puts slavery in a context in which we look beyond its immediate reality of oppression to the more pleasing reality of freedom that came later, which maybe is always the inevitable direction of things. Another odd occurrence is the narrator's revelation of a supernatural event involving the man who eventually married Caldonia's personal attendant, Loretta. He was a sailor who spent a lot of time at sea, and one day he saw two sailors simply disappear while he was talking to another sailor (319). One general point is that Loretta will go on to marry after slavery. Another is that there are many forces affecting reality that are larger than slavery. One larger reality is that black people did survive slavery, and perhaps all Americans will eventually transcend its negative legacy.

The narrator is always concerned with creating a context to critique slavery. No matter how one interprets the specifics of the odd portrayals, the irony, and the humor, one should remember that this is consistently the narrator's intent.

The shortest chapter, chapter 11, takes a timeline from Tuesday at the end of chapter 10 to Sunday of the next week, with several of the narrator's typical revelations of the future interspersed; entitled "A Mule Stands Up. Of Cadavers and Kisses and Keys. An American Poet Speaks of Poland and Mortality.," the chapter's portrayal is very much characteristic of the style of the rest of the novel. The major event in the chapter is the murder on Wednesday of Augustus by a man in Georgia when Augustus refuses to work after the man buys him[9] (343–47). Also, that Thursday, Caldonia makes Elias overseer in place of Moses. Celeste finds this out on Friday (354), creating tension between her and Elias because of his hatred of Moses, and because he becomes overseer in his place (350–51). The revelations about the change in Stamford since his supernatural experience in the storm and his future after slavery are significant (351–54). Also, the section corresponding to "An American Poet Speaks of Poland and Mortality" (355–57) is not as humorous as others, but it is still a similarly odd, ironic portrayal that creates a context to critique slavery. The main part of the ironic portrayal that engages attention and directs it to close scrutiny of slavery is a word used in an insurance policy on slaves: "there will be no protection . . . on the perishment of your human property" (356–57). "Perishment" is an odd-sounding word, a word that might apply to perishable produce, for example, and its use is ironic because one would not expect it to apply to "human property."[10] Oddly, unexpectedly, the man who used the word was from Poland and was "something of a poet." Connecting this chapter to chapter 12, the penultimate sentence reads in part: "All of Caldonia's guests [Fern, Dora, and Louis who arrived Thursday (349)], except her mother, would stay [through Saturday] until Sunday" (357).

Chapter 12 is not greatly different, but it does have a relatively clear chronology. Its main focus is the events of "Sunday" that bring what happened in the immediate aftermath of Henry's death in 1855 to a close. "Sunday" is the first part of the chapter's title, and one of the least ironic title elements in the novel.

Because it puts together a series of events to move to a close, the first of six episodes in chapter 12 is its longest, fifteen pages. At the beginning, John remembers what Elias has said about Moses being "world stupid" (359) and finally figures out where he is hiding. He must be at Mildred's: the "place was on the way south, the opposite of where a runaway slave might want to be," but being "world stupid" and not knowing one direction from the other, Moses ended up there because he thought he was going north. John goes there to arrest Moses and ends up murdering Mildred (363–65); Counsel murders John (368–69); Counsel arrests Moses (370–71); and on slave patrol, Oden Peoples severs Moses's Achilles tendon because he ran away (372–74). After he hobbles Moses, Oden realizes he cannot make Louis, who has come on the scene along Elias, carry Moses on his horse because he is Robbins's son (376). This is another nuance in slavery's hierarchy. Although in many instances Oden the Cherokee would be higher and more powerful in the hierarchy than free black people like Louis, here Oden does not have the same power because Louis is the free black son of a powerful white man. The cutting of Moses's Achilles tendon points ahead to the very last section of the novel, after chapter 12, that depicts a permanently disabled Moses, although the fate of the others who ran away from slavery is by no means the same.

Chapter 12 ends with a section that is a good segue to the sections following the chapter. "Finding a Lost Loved One" (380–82), the third part of the chapter's title, is the story of Minerva deserting Winifred in Philadelphia "three years and nine months after John Skiffington was killed" (380). Winifred puts out wanted posters with Minerva's name and description on them: "'Lost Or Harmed In Some Unknown Way On The Streets Of This City—A Precious Loved One.' . . . But at the bottom of the posters, like some kind of afterthought, in words much smaller than anything else on the poster, was the line 'Will Answer to The Name Minnie'" (381). Winifred thought that she "loved Minerva more than she loved any other human being in the world" (382) and meant no harm by the wording of the posters. However, because of these words, Minerva refuses to go back to Winifred to explain why she left.

The words "finding a lost loved one" draw attention to their underlying meaning in what happens between Winifred and Minerva. The words that offend Minerva and cause the breach between her and Winifred go back to the day of Winifred's wedding. Giving Minerva as a present, Belle Skiffington tells Winifred that her "[proper] name is Minerva" (32), but she "will answer to the name Minnie. . . . [or] whatever you choose to call her" (32). At the time Minerva only curtsies, and perhaps the significance of Belle's words and being a slave do not register with her. However, all these years later, even after the benign treatment she has received from the Skiffingtons, Minerva finds that she resents her life as a slave, symbolized in the words of Belle on the wedding day—"will answer to the name Minnie"—and repeated by Winifred on the poster. In spite of everything, slavery has not been all right with her, and now she will live as a free woman without explaining anything to her former mistress. A slave named in the oppressive, dehumanizing, belittling words of a slave owner, whether it is Belle who supports slavery or Winifred who does not (33), can never be a "loved one" to the slave owner; Minerva has never been a "loved one" to John and Winifred Skiffington. Winifred can never "find" what she never had or "lost"; Minerva is never going back to her.

The story of Minerva living a free life in Philadelphia ends chapter 12 because it connects well to the last three unnumbered episodes that show other ex-slaves from Manchester County living free in Washington, D.C., and Celeste, still a slave on Caldonia's plantation, transcending slavery spiritually and psychologically. The three final sections emphasize the novel's main theme of black people's triumph over slavery.

The first two ending episodes depict liberation through the lives of ex-slaves in Washington and in the artistic vision of Alice, which Calvin, writing to Caldonia on April 12, 1861, the date of the start of the Civil War, shows is similar to the omniscient narrator's. Calvin finds Alice, Priscilla, and Jamie living free at a hotel in Washington (383–86). He affirms the black freedom he finds in Washington through the positive description of the characters, their lives, and the community: "*All that is here is owned by Alice, Priscilla and all the people who work here, many of them, to be sure, runaways. . . . Jamie comes and goes as a student in a school for colored children. He is as fine a young man as any father or mother could want*" (386). Using the context of his past, he further affirms black freedom in his letter: "*What I feared most* [was that] . . . *they would remember my history, that I, no matter what I had always said to the contrary, owned people of our Race. I feared that they would send me away, and even as I write you now, I am still afraid.*"

Two artworks by Alice that she has signed "Alice Night" (384–85) are central in the first two ending sections. Calvin describes the first as "*a grand piece of art that is part tapestry, part painting, and part clay structure—all in one exquisite Creation. . . . It is a map of life made with every kind of art man has ever thought to represent himself. Yes, clay. Yes, paint. Yes, cloth. There are no people . . . just all the houses and barns and roads and cemeteries and wells in our Manchester. It is what God sees when he looks down on Manchester*" (384). The second work portrays "*your* [Caldonia's] *plantation, and again, it is what God sees when He looks down. There is nothing missing, not a cabin, not a barn, not a chicken, not a horse. Not a single person is missing. I suspect that if I were to count the blades of grass, the number would be correct as it was once when the creator of this work knew that world*" (385). Alice's godlike artistic vision of an eclectic, inviolable wholeness clearly implies freedom, just as the omniscient narrator's vision does,[11] just as that of Edward P. Jones, the novel's godlike creator of characters, does. Alice's perseverance, "playing crazy" for a long time to map the county and get a chance to escape, is not the same quality as her godlike artistry, but the two qualities work together. Not all slaves are artists like Alice but, similar to Alice, there is in many of them a strong, although perhaps unconscious, imaginary vision which coalesces with perseverance in the pursuit of freedom.

Maybe the most outstanding example of a slave becoming "free" is Celeste, who transcends slavery spiritually and psychologically although she is still legally a slave. In the last two-page, unnumbered episode, Caldonia reads Calvin's letter over and over and shares it with her new husband, Louis Cartwright ("the last name Louis's mother, Philomena, had chosen for herself and her children" [107]). Louis says that she may "wear out the paper" with all the reading (387). She says, "By then . . . I will have memorized every word and will be ready for the next letter." Caldonia even reads the letter at Henry's grave, but on her way back to the house, she sees Moses limping back to his cabin and "found it difficult to move after seeing him." So apparently Caldonia starts to understand something about the importance of freedom, and literally sees the horror of slavery too. Celeste is the ultimate example of love and kindness that will always transcend de jure slavery, though. Even after Moses's meanness and cruelty toward her and her family, she, still also a slave as he is, sends his meals to him every day by her children: "Her meals to Moses would be until the end," and even after Moses was dead, "Celeste was never to close down her days . . . without thinking aloud at least once to everyone and yet to no one in particular, 'I wonder if Moses done ate yet'" (388).

Celeste's spiritual and psychological transcendence of de jure slavery evolves to de facto freedom through the free lives of her children, and although Elias is not as good an example of transcendence as Celeste, the future lives of their children also represent his influence and relate to his life.[12] The narrator reveals that Tessie dies in 1946 at the age of ninety-seven with a doll near her that Elias made for her when she was six and a slave (67, 350). She obviously outlives slavery by many, many decades, and dies as a free woman with Elias "on her mind all that dying morning" (350). Celeste and Elias's son Elwood is an even stronger symbol of freedom that evolves from the legacy of his parents. The narrator also looks ahead twenty years to 1875 when a free Elwood will meet Stamford in Richmond to become a teacher at Stamford's Richmond Home for Colored Orphans. Thus the narrator shows that Elwood will work very constructively to help black people when he is free, in a sense connecting specifically with the positive efforts of his mother and extending her "freedom" through transcendence of slavery to make it de facto freedom. As slaves, Elias and Celeste never have a surname, but the surname that the children apparently choose, along with the proliferation of their family, emphasize and highlight the idea of creating a legacy that leads to de facto freedom: "The generations of Celeste and Elias Freemen would be legion in Virginia" (351).

This ending of the novel is a statement of how indefatigable the idea of freedom is in black people. Some like Henry, Moses, and Caldonia get lost and stray along the way, but what we see in Celeste, first and foremost, and also in Alice and Elias more than compensates for what happens to Henry, Moses, and Caldonia, confirming the point about freedom. Further, Augustus and Mildred die, but the example of their quest for freedom is unforgettable. Because he changes and goes on to leave a great legacy, the example of Stamford is outstanding, too. Fern is freeborn and not even black in appearance. However, because Jebediah Dickson makes her feel that she belongs to him instead of him belonging to her (286), she also develops an understanding of the importance of freedom, and reveals it in her transformation to empathy for slaves and their freedom quest. Finally, Barnum Kinsey shows that even a poor white drunk, someone very low in slavery's hierarchy, can have the desire to treat black people fairly, his racist attitudes engendered by slavery notwithstanding. Maybe everyone, therefore, can evolve to accept the idea of black freedom and equality.

CHAPTER 3

The Known World's Characters

The Amistad paperback edition of *The Known World* lists forty-five characters; also, throughout the novel the godlike omniscient narrator tells stories featuring a veritable multitude of additional characters, stories about slavery in 1855, the time of the novel's beginning and the year of its central setting, stories that are also often proleptic and analeptic. Along with disparate, fragmentary narrative and thematic elements and a loosely connected central narrative, the large number of characterizations encompassing the past, present, and future symbolize a historical whole, a totality of African American experience. The dominant theme of the novel is black people's triumph over slavery and oppression, and although some black men are very important in this context, arguably black women are more prominent in this portrayal of the triumph of black humanity. It is only an educated speculation that Jones's great love and respect for his mother influenced his portrayal of black women;[1] however, whatever the reason may be, a number of black women stand out in the novel above everyone, black and white, as examples of remarkable human beings who overcame the unbelievable travail of slavery, preparing the way for freedom.

Black Female Characters in *The Known World*

Among the listed characters who play roles in the loosely connected 1855 central story about the death of black slave owner Henry Townsend and its aftermath, in the novel's whole multitude of characters, Celeste is the most remarkable human being. This is ironic because she has a permanent limp, which makes even her husband, Elias, pity her before he discovers his love and they marry (78–79), and which impels another slave to tell her once that she should be shot like a horse with a broken leg (100). She so greatly transcends her affliction, however, that it only highlights how remarkable she is. Part of the evidence of her outstanding character resides in the dignity she shows in resisting slavery, even though others see her as lowly, befitting a slave, and even lowly among slaves. An example is what she says to Elias when he accepts his black owner Caldonia's request to become overseer to spite the hated black former overseer Moses after he escapes, to show Moses when "they bring [him] back . . . how the world went on without him" (336). Celeste reminds him: "It just ain't right to go and do what they bought you for. Why make it easy?" Not only is slavery wrong, but slaves should not accommodate it in any way.

Also, she rebels against slavery in subtle ways; earlier in the novel, the narrator says that Celeste's "small way of saying no to everything" (79) was to call Henry and Caldonia "Mr." and "Ma'am" instead of "Master" and "Mistress." However, although Celeste hates slavery, she never hates other slaves; it is her remarkable ability to love and forgive other slaves who are themselves the victims of slavery's pernicious system that projects her to a unique level of importance. (Again, it is only speculation, but it seems that the characterization of Celeste as a person who suffered greatly and turned her suffering into love and caring for other people might relate to what Jones saw in the life of his beloved mother, who loved him and her other children so much and overcame so much, in spite of her great hardship.)[2]

Celeste's loving forgiveness starts with Elias and extends to Moses, the one whom she could hate most because he has always expressed hostility toward Elias and, most memorably, makes her work in the fields when she is six-months pregnant and causes her to miscarry (326–27). Regarding Elias and his hatred for Moses and taking over as overseer after Moses's escape, "Celeste did not know what she was going to do with Elias. She loved him, and no matter what there would be no way to get around that. Everything else that came their way—even his hatred of Moses—would have to do battle with her love for him. She could only hope that Elias would find his way back to what he had been" (351). After all he has done to hurt her, she empathizes with and implies love for her fellow slave Moses after his escape: "She was thinking that such a lovely day could only mean that they would kill poor Moses when they found him. The God of that Bible, being who he was, never gave a slave a good day without wanting something big in return" (337). Interestingly, Celeste does not seem to ground her love in the Bible, but she is probably thinking about the Bible as taught by the free lackey black preacher Valtims Moffett, paid by slave owners to preach to slaves to obey their masters (87). On the contrary, her love fits the standard of true Christianity that is above that of ersatz Christian slave owners. In the very last paragraph of the novel, Celeste continues to love and take care of Moses after slave catchers have punished him by permanently injuring him and bringing him back to the plantation (388). The focus on Celeste's loving actions in the last paragraph implies that she is the most important human example in the novel.

After Celeste, Alice and Mildred Townsend are the next two very prominent women characters. Alice perhaps deserves discussion first because her quest for freedom is so unshakable, because her vision which supports this quest is the novel's focus near the end just before it concludes with the paragraph referring to Celeste.[3] Alice's quest and vision are a specific symbolic representation of everything, a historical whole, a totality of African American experience within the novel's larger body of characterizations and general structure that symbolize the same thing.

For a long time, Alice makes everyone, the other slaves, all the white people, and everyone in Manchester County, think she is "crazy"; they believe her story, told in her "very rare" "saner moments" (4), that on a "plantation in a faraway county whose name only she remembered" a mule kicked her in the head. Alice works hard and does nothing abnormal in the fields during the day (269), but because everyone accepts that she is crazy, in the night the white slave patrollers do not stop her from wandering all over the county doing things unacceptable for any other slave. On one occasion when she encounters the patrollers, "Alice lifted her frock and danced and tried to climb onto the horse with one man" (271) before the patrollers "charged off," leaving her alone. However, her craziness is only a strategy in her ongoing, never-ending quest for freedom; Alice is only "map[ing] her way again and again through the night" (295) so that she will know Manchester County well when she gets an opportunity to escape. Moses has been following Alice at night and observing how she takes "note of all around her" (272). He finally figures out that she is not crazy, that maybe someone "could just be crazy by pretending to be crazy for a long, long time." Alice gets her opportunity to escape when Moses proposes that she run away with his wife, Priscilla, and son Jamie (295), his delusional intention being to marry black plantation owner Caldonia (292–93). When the time comes for the escape, Alice drops the crazy posture. When Priscilla cries because she is afraid, Alice slaps her and takes charge so that the escape will not fail. "Not one tear ever watered my thirst, and it won't water yours neither. So stop it all right now" (297). "Who was this new woman, who was this Alice acting like this in the night?" Alice is not "new"; she is the same Alice who has been there all along, feigning craziness. Alice and the escapees then disappear into the night, only to be seen again at the end of the novel when they are free in Washington, D.C..

At the end, Alice's two artistic creations that depict literally everything in Manchester County and everything and *everyone* on Henry and Caldonia's plantation, those now living and those now dead (384–86), represent her symbolic vision of the black experience that is also the novel's. Living free in Washington, Alice implies the inevitability of freedom expressed in her vision when she responds to freeborn black character Calvin Newman's statement that he hopes she has been well: "I been good as God keeps me" (386). In the final analysis, freedom for *everyone* is inevitable because it comes from God.

Given first her "crazy" antics and then later her abrupt change to "normality," Alice perhaps seems more a symbol than a realistically portrayed character, and Celeste, who has a physical disability and loves her family and others, seems more a realistic portrayal. However, many black people (Elias for example) share the quest and vision that are specific and individual in Alice, and many stick to their vision and pursue freedom as relentlessly as Alice. Overall, both Celeste and Alice, along with all the other characters and structural elements of the novel, are part of a mosaic symbolizing black life that inevitably progresses to freedom.

Although her life circumstances and the outcome of her life are different, Mildred Townsend is generally similar to Celeste: she shows great courage and moral strength and maintains her ability to love and her human dignity from the hardships of slavery to the successive perils of freedom, and she dies unjustly while showing compassion, dignity, and courage in freedom. Along with her husband, Augustus, after he has bought his freedom and then hers, Mildred demonstrates her loving commitment to their son Henry by going every Sunday to visit him for approximately ten years until Augustus can buy Henry's freedom, too (17–19, 44–50). During the years before his freedom, Henry strangely starts to become enamored of his white master William Robbins, and this distracts his attention from his parents, causing him to show up late and sometimes not to show up at all to meet them on cold Sundays. Understandably, Augustus becomes exasperated, and one day he angrily pushes Henry to the ground when he arrives late. Although Augustus dearly loves Henry, Mildred's response distinguishes her motherly, female love from Augustus's: "Henry covered his face and began to cry. 'Augustus!' Mildred shouted and helped her son up. 'Everything's good,' she said to him as she cradled him in her arms. 'Everything's good'" (19). Later, after Augustus and Henry have a physical confrontation after the latter is free and then buys his own slave, Mildred's response is similar when the men separate in anger: "Mildred followed [Henry]. 'Please, son, please.' . . . 'Henry. Wait, son.' . . . His mother came out into the yard and watched him go away in the dark. For a long time she could hear the horse moving on what passed for a road out where they were and the sounds of his going away gave her an image of him in her mind that stayed with her for days" (138–39).

After Henry's death and after slave patrollers sell the legally free Augustus back into slavery, Mildred shows compassion for the escaped Moses by taking him in and hiding him; at the same time, while waiting for Sheriff John Skiffington to find Augustus, but knowing instinctively that she will never see him again, she courageously tries to protect Moses when the sheriff comes to arrest him. Mildred comes to the door with her rifle in moral indignation because slavery has wrongly taken Augustus and is now trying to reclaim Moses too. "Come to tell me what I already know bout my husband, sheriff?' (364). "[You will take no] more [black men]. No more men from here. No more men from anywhere. Not no more." After Skiffington shoots her, the narrator describes her dreamlike transition into death that implies her legacy of love in life: "It was late and she had been somewhere she could not remember. She went into [her] dark house and up the stairs and found the door to Henry's room open. [Caldonia told her that Henry] was resting quite well. Henry did not stir as his mother looked down on him and Mildred was grateful for that. She left the room and found Augustus in their bed, also asleep, and she got in and made herself comfortable in his arms. . . . She closed her eyes and pulled Augustus's arm closer about her and closed her eyes"[4] (365–66). Also, after her death, Moses, the previously mean, callous overseer, feels gratitude for her help. "She had asked him not one question, just gave him a home" (370). Moses tells sheriff's deputy Counsel Skiffington, who has just killed the sheriff: '"I don't wanna leave Miss Mildred out here on the floor like this, Mister'" (371). "He knew he was grateful to her and so as he [cleaned up blood] he thanked Mildred for helping him and then he picked up her body and laid her out on the table" (374).

Whereas these black women characters' unchanging attributes stand out in an immoral world which has lost its direction, Fern Elston is a black woman who changes from supporting slavery to accepting and respecting the humanity of slaves; her change in adult life is one that happened far too infrequently and speaks volumes about her inner human fiber. The fact that Fern is a light-enough-to-pass-for-white (74), freeborn, slave-owning black woman who really has no external impetus for her moral change shows how impressive she is.

Fern's change occurs when she develops empathy for a slave named Jebediah Dickson, who undergoes suffering because he refuses to accept that he is anything but a human being who is the equal of others. Several episodes in the novel describe Fern's encounter with Dickson, who has free papers but is a slave in spite of denying it (248–61). A gambler, Jebediah initially confronts Fern because her husband Ramsey, who is away gambling, owes him money that he demands from her. After this, a series of events occur: already starting to change, Fern buys Jebediah from his owner; she has one of her other slaves beat him until he is unconscious for insulting her (259); working on Fern's land, Jebediah steps on a rusty nail and has to have his foot amputated (259–60). The crucial point is when Fern, clearly feeling for Jebediah now, draws up manumission papers to free him: not having written the word "manumit" before, she misspells it and Jebediah corrects her; she then feels that, among "all the human beings she would ever know in her life, he would be the only one she would come close to saying 'I am sorry' to" (260).

She is in the process of freeing him anyway but, apparently coming to full realization of his literacy, which in this specific instance is superior to hers, she reaches the high point of her moral development. She understands finally that, although a slave, Jebediah is a human being who has a right that all other human beings have. He has the right to acquire literacy (his master's wife taught him) and take advantage of it to move freely throughout life like any free person. She accepts literacy as the right of all people, including all slaves. After her experience with Jebediah, "she was never to see the world the same way again" (73), and when she went to Caldonia's plantation after Henry's death, she no longer refused to "mingle with 'any slave that was not house broken.'" Fern, a thirty-four-year-old woman (257) who has grown up having the highest privilege among black people in the slave system, thereby shows an ability to empathize, grow, and change in the face of the powerful immoral force of slavery, revealing herself to be a remarkable character.[5]

William Robbins's black mistress Philomena Cartwright does not have the clearly positive characterization of the women above; however, a combination of childlike fantasy and realistic practicality, she plays a role in transgressing the boundaries of slavery and working to attain freedom for herself, her family, and a friend. Born on the plantation of rich white Robert Colfax, Philomena had a desire to live in a fantastical Richmond that among its many wonders had "fireworks [displays] every night" (114–15); starting when she was eight, she developed this vision of Richmond from the stories that another slave on Colfax's plantation, Sophie, told her. However, after Robbins sees and buys her from Colfax, she also uses Robbins's attraction to her to get him to give her a house with a maid, to free her, to buy her mother and brother and give them to her as slaves, and to buy and give her Sophie, who told the stories she liked so much. Philomena's brother and Sophie manage to escape, with the help of Philomena, the novel clearly implies, and Robbins never catches them. Philomena also uses the occasion of the birth of their first child, Dora, to start violating the rules of black-white relationships in the slave system. She starts calling Robbins by his first name, "William," saying sometimes, "You don't be treatin me right, William. You just don't, William" (116). She later goes even further by slapping him back when he slaps her after he comes to get her when she runs away to Richmond, trying to find the place of her fantasies (117). (Robbins then punches her in the jaw with his fist so hard that she never again could "eat hard food on that side of her mouth" [144]).

Philomena is fanciful and childlike and takes great abuse from Robbins, who later asserts temporary control over her by threatening to sell her back into slavery, although she has her free papers (144–45); however, she still strikes a blow against slavery in her violation of its boundaries and especially in the steps she takes to free her brother and Sophie, first essentially and then literally, and her mother, essentially. Philomena sees Richmond for a final time when it is burning during the Civil War: "The fires were still smoldering in Richmond when Philomena got there that last time, and she commented to Louis and Dora and Caldonia and her grandson [Robbins] that the fires on the ground were poor substitutes for fireworks in the air [from the stories Sophie told her]." It seems that the fantasy of Richmond may still be in her mind, and here and nowhere else does the novel suggest that Philomena is a character who is as serious and committed to freedom as Celeste, Alice, and Mildred. Nevertheless, in this scene her own freedom to go where she wants and the black freedom that is coming after the Civil War correspond with her efforts to bring about freedom throughout her earlier life, and her characterization is largely positive.

Although the novel does not develop them fully enough to make a clear evaluation, two other black females who have significantly positive characteristics are William Robbins's black daughter Dora Cartwright, his child with Philomena, and John and Winifred Skiffington's slave Minerva. Although she is the black child of the richest white man in Manchester County and has privilege because of this, there is nothing clearly negative about Dora. What is clearly good is that, in spite of having witnessed him abuse her mother (118), and in spite of never having been to his plantation before (362), she goes there to help take care of him after he has a stroke because she loves him. When her white half-sister Patience Robbins answers the door, she says, "I would like to see Mr. Robbins, please." Recognizing that the woman must be her sister because she looks just like her, Patience "knew almost immediately that standing before her was the only other person who loved William Robbins the way she did. She had been carrying the weight of his illness alone, and as she stood there, she felt the burden grow less and less" (363). The novel goes into even less depth in its portrayal of Minerva. However, it is clear that, near the end when she is a free woman (381–82), it is positive that she rejects the diminution of her humanity symbolized in her naming as a slave: "She will answer to the name Minnie, but her proper name is Minerva. She will, however, answer to either, to whatever you choose to call her" (32).

Moses's wife, Priscilla, is a black woman slave who, in clear contrast to Celeste and Mildred, is initially weak-minded and indecisive, but the experience of freedom causes a total positive transformation in her by the end. For most of the novel, Priscilla is a pretty pathetic person because she was "weighed down with worshipping her husband [Moses] and her mistress [Caldonia]" (295). Because she worships Moses, he takes advantage by abusing her: "He slapped her. It was not a hard hit but she went to her knees nevertheless because the slap came with years of abuse and rejection" (263). Priscilla only pitifully pleads with Moses: "Why you gotta treat me this way, Moses? Why you can't do right by me?" Later, because she worships Caldonia and because she is psychologically subservient to the slave system Caldonia represents, she is afraid to escape from slavery, and Alice has to slap her, to shock sense into her, to make her run away to freedom (297). By the end when Caldonia's twin brother Calvin sees her, however (384–86), it is obvious that she is working with Alice as a free woman in Washington, D.C., to affirm freedom in a community of black people, "many of them, to be sure, runaways" (386). Calvin's description makes her positive change clear: "I turned and saw Moses's Priscilla. Her hands were confidently behind her back, her clothing impeccable. I knew in those few seconds that whatever she had been in Virginia, she was that no more" (385).

Among the black women, Caldonia is probably the most enigmatic, but she is also one of the most negatively portrayed because she is so superficial and selfish. One of the novel's early indications of Caldonia's flaws is Augustus's thoughts about her following Henry's death when, instead of freeing her slaves, she tells them that "God stands with us" (64). Augustus had always thought that in her, although a free-born woman from a slave-owning family, he saw "a light . . . that had failed in his own son born into slavery. But the light was not in her words" (64–65).

Her sexual relationship with Moses after Henry's death is a strong indication of just how superficial and selfish Caldonia is, though.[6] The relationship with Moses starts with his accounts each evening about the slaves' daily activities in the fields that turn, at Caldonia's request, into stories about Henry (208–9). Moses's stories quickly become very fanciful: "Caldonia had her head back and her eyes closed, which had been her way since the second evening. He had begun to feel that he could say anything and it would not matter" (262). Maybe Caldonia wants to hear fanciful stories about Henry because she still loves him after his death. However, this is not clear because her sexual relationship with Moses calls her love for Henry into question.

It does seem clear that she lacks depth of human feeling, and thus sees Moses as only someone inferior to her on social and human levels, someone she can use for her own sexual gratification and to give herself some strange sense of comfort. When Moses left after sex one night, Caldonia "said to herself . . . 'I love Moses. I love Moses with his one name.' But when she saw [her house slave attendant] Loretta, the words did not make as much sense. 'I am ready for bed,' she said, and that made the greatest sense. Before going to bed, she washed her insides with vinegar and the soap her slaves made for everyone. Hers, however, was made with a dash of perfume that Loretta supplied to the soap makers" (292). The last sentence indicates superficial self-centeredness. The more important point though is that she does not really love Moses as she muses to herself; she only has the need for the comforting image of his one-name inferiority, an image which also causes her contradictorily to feel that she needs cleansing after sex with him. Caldonia then manipulates Moses into thinking that she will free him (324–25), causing him to run away when she does not (330–35), leading to his being captured and hobbled (371–74). The last thing the novel tells us about this relationship is that, when Caldonia sees Moses on one occasion, back on her plantation, still her slave, now always limping, "Her heart stopped. Even years after their last encounter, her heart stopped" (387). She feels some remorse or regret for Moses, but this is not nearly enough to explain her earlier dehumanization of him and her still enslaving him.

There are two sections alluding to black people's imminent freedom that could possibly cast Caldonia in a more positive light. One is the description of her viewing Richmond burning during the Civil War with her new husband, Louis; mother-in-law, Philomena; and sister-in-law Dora (144–45). The other, just before the quotation above showing her observing Moses, is the description of her standing before the grave of her first husband, slave-owning Henry, reading her twin brother Calvin's letter, written on the day the Civil War began, celebrating black freedom in Washington (387). Freedom is already a reality in Washington, freedom is coming in Richmond and the South, and Caldonia is moving into the era of American freedom, but it is not clear that she ever changes as a person (as Fern does, for example). Like the reference to her emotional reaction to seeing Moses hobbled and limping, these scenes are not enough clearly to mitigate the negativity of Caldonia's characterization. She remains an enigma, but one who is more negative than anything else.

It is not clear in the novel that this is true either, but maybe Caldonia takes her negative character traits from her mother, Maude Newman, a slave-owning black woman so selfish and ruthless that she poisons her husband, Caldonia's father, Tilmon, to stop him from selling their slaves, whom she calls their economic legacy (66, 184–85). While many things about Caldonia are not clear, it is clear that Maude is absolutely the worst among the black women characters in the loosely connected central story about Henry's 1855 death, and one of the worst characters in the entire novel. Caldonia and her mother's characterizations do not diminish the very positive characterizations of several black women, but they do provide some balance.

White Female Characters in *The Known World*

Several of the white women characters that play roles in the loosely connected central story of the death of black slave owner Henry Townsend and its aftermath are hopelessly corrupted by slavery's ideology or lost in its poisonous fog. Among the white women, Belle Skiffington, wife of the nefarious Counsel Skiffington, the woman who gives the slave Minerva as a wedding gift to Counsel's cousin John and his bride, Winifred (31–32), is probably the worst. "Her first maid [the second maid is in the backyard with Minerva before Belle presents her to Winifred], received when Belle was twelve, had had a disagreeable night cough and had to be replaced after a few weeks with a quieter soul." An aristocratic white woman, Belle thinks nothing of owning a slave or giving one as a gift because black people are replaceable, dispensable objects to her.

Instead of being turned into evil human beings by slavery's influence as Belle is, two other white women characters, Winifred and Clara Martin, respectively, become an accommodationist for slavery, at best, and hopelessly bewildered by its ideology. They are different but not clearly better.

The portrayal of Winifred is subtle and somewhat ambiguous, but in the final analysis she is an accommodationist if not a proponent of slavery. Winifred is from Philadelphia and apparently opposes slavery because she went to the Philadelphia School for Girls, which had associations with antislavery Quakerism (30), but her opposition is not clear. Regardless of whether she opposes slavery at first, however, she allows her husband, John, to persuade her that Minerva will live a good life with them as a slave because they are good people (33–35). Later, in spite of John's objection, Winifred cannot "help herself" (280) and teaches Minerva to read in what could be an attempt to defy the rules of slavery and improve her life. However, Winifred "had only asked that Minerva not let anyone see her reading." Teaching Minerva to read probably does not mean that Winifred accepts her as a human being with the right to a good life, as it might seem. The fact that Winifred does not want anyone outside the family to see Minerva read is more likely part of the process of accommodating herself to slavery. In this context, she adheres to the dictates of slavery publicly and turns Minerva into her own private creation, a reading slave, in an attempt to assuage her own conscience. When Winifred later puts out the wanted poster for Minerva in Philadelphia (380–82), her use of the same language referring to Minerva's demeaning naming as a slave that Belle uses when she gives her as a gift supports the idea that she has become an accommodationist, as does Minerva's rejection of Winifred when she tries to get her back in Philadelphia.

Winifred's Manchester County, Virginia, cousin Clara Martin is so confused by slavery's ideology that she has lost touch with what she truly feels and wants. Talking to John Skiffington, Clara calls her slave Ralph a "possible miscreant" and asks John to talk to him not because of anything bad that he does, but because she becomes paranoid one day when *she* feels sexual attraction to him after allowing him to touch her hand and comb her hair, which she is having trouble doing (150–53). After talking to Ralph, John assures Clara that she has nothing to fear (154). The narrator looks ahead twenty years to the time of the Civil War and afterwards when Ralph stays with Clara because she convinces him the place will not be the same without him. In spite of asking him to stay, to protect herself from him supposedly, Clara locks and then nails her door shut each night until she dies, after which Ralph has nowhere to go and moves in with relatives in Washington, D.C.. The narrator never says what Ralph knows about all of this or how it makes him feel, and does not indicate that Clara harms him psychologically. This notwithstanding, Clara is a white woman laughably confused by slavery's ideology of race.[7]

The only possible exceptions to the negative characterizations of white women are William Robbins's wife and daughter, Ethel and Patience, but their portrayals are not full enough to be conclusive. It seems good that Patience loves her father and accepts her black sister, whom she has never seen before but knows is her sister because they look alike and she sees the same love for their father in her eyes that she feels (362–63), but it is not possible to reach any conclusions from this. Also, perhaps Patience's name symbolizes her virtue, but this is only a guess because the novel does not develop her in sufficient depth to support it. The novel gives few specific details about Patience beyond those in the scene with Dora, and the generally scant description of her does not portray her as clearly good or bad. All we essentially know about Ethel is that she no longer loves William Robbins and will not help him during his illness because of his sexual dalliances. This is not bad, but neither does it reveal anything that is necessarily good about her. Her portrayal is more inconclusive than her daughter's.

Black Male Characters in *The Known World*

Among the black male characters, Henry's father Augustus Townsend and Elias are the two most positively portrayed, and there is not much, if anything, to raise one above the other. Although neither displays love as unfailing as Celeste or Mildred Townsend in adverse circumstances, they love others, especially their families, significantly and pursue freedom with a tenacity comparable to

Alice's. Overall, they are both outstanding men who are lovers as well as models of the unquenchable desire for freedom, human dignity, and family stability while enslaved in an unimaginably horrible system.

The magnitude of his perseverance to attain his freedom and that of his family and determination to remain free in spite of the slave system's intransigence are what stand out most about Augustus. He works to buy his freedom from William Robbins (14–17), works about three more years to buy Mildred's, and approximately ten more years to buy Henry's (44–50). Nothing stops him, although slavery's embodiment, Robbins, puts every possible obstacle in his way and terribly exploits him economically in the sale of Henry (17).

Augustus never gives up on freedom and, because of who he is as a person, his spirit will always be free, when slave patrollers illegally sell him to kidnappers who re-enslave and resell him, when his new owner shoots him and he dies. The slave patrollers have to compel Augustus to go with the slave speculators, his kidnappers, by gunpoint (214), and one of the kidnappers has to beat Augustus to make him comply (216). Augustus continues to resist his kidnappers along the way as they travel south trying to sell him, once pretending to be deaf and dumb in South Carolina so that a man will not buy him (277–78). When they finally succeed in selling him in Georgia, his buyer, Hillard Uster, says "I don't want no trouble"; Augustus replies, "I won't be nothin but trouble" (344–45). In reply to Hillard's statement that he just wants to feed his family, Augustus says, "I know family. I know all about family. But, mister, you can't raise your family on my back" (345). Then "Augustus, noting where the sun was, turned and headed north." Hillard shoots him and, according to the narrator, when Augustus died" in Georgia near the Florida line, he rose up above the barn where he had died . . . and he walked away quick-like, toward Virginia. . . . He came to the house he had built for his family, for Mildred his wife and Henry his son, and he opened and went through the door. . . . Then he went to [Mildred's] bed, leaned over and kissed her left breast" (346–47). "The kiss went through the breast . . . and came to the cage that protected the heart. Now the kiss, like so many kisses . . . was forgetful, and it could not find the right key to the cage. So in the end, frustrated, desperate, the kiss squeezed through the bars and kissed Mildred's heart."[8] Mildred then realizes that her loving husband is dead and rises and stumbles outside in unfathomable pain.

Augustus is great, and his few negative actions in the novel reduce his greatness only minimally. He acts badly twice, once when he pushes Henry to the ground when he shows up late for one of the Sunday visits before Augustus buys his freedom (19), and once when he hits Henry on the shoulder with a cane, breaking his shoulder, when Henry tells his parents he has bought a slave

(137–39). Both of these acts are violent, but Augustus is terribly frustrated that his son seems to understand none of the gravity of slavery and slave owning and seems not to appreciate any of Augustus's arduous efforts to attain freedom for him and the family. Both acts by a former slave who has gone through what Augustus has are understandable. Augustus's love for Henry is not flawless and transcendent like his wife, Mildred's, and his love and the overall quality of his character do not reach the level of Celeste's. However, the love for Henry and Mildred that he still exhibits and his death right before Mildred's near the end, in the same quest for freedom as hers, place him on a plane close to her as an exemplar.

Elias chooses love of Celeste over trying to escape to freedom, greatly loves his family, and develops emotional ties to a slave boy named Luke that are just like love; it is his decision to hate Moses that turns out to be a great mistake. Elias attempts to escape from Henry's plantation, and William Robbins captures him (78–81), but after this he still plans to escape (98). It is then that Elias has the feeling of wanting to be with Celeste, and does not know why. He only knows that he hurts when he sees her, and hears "the sound of her limping down the lane . . . the front of her bad leg scraping along in that second before she lifted it." He loves her although he does not know it at first, and he decides to propose to her and ask Henry to let them marry. He does this although, as Henry also well knows when he agrees to the marriage, it precludes his running away in the future because he will now be married to a crippled woman who cannot run anywhere (99–102). But Elias never regrets loving Celeste or the fact that marrying her stops him from running away.[9]

Elias also loves his children by Celeste, and they love him. The narrator tells a story about Elias's daughter Tessie that strongly implies his love for her and hers for him. On her dying day about ninety years after the present time of the novel, she thinks about Elias and a doll he made for her: "Her father had been on her mind all that dying morning, and she asked one of her great-grandchildren to go to the attic and find the doll" (350). Further, before his own children are born, a slave boy named Luke comforts Elias after his escape attempt, and Elias becomes as close to Luke "as any human being could be to the man's heart" (97). Luke also lives with Elias and Celeste after they marry, and when Henry hires Luke out and a man works him to death, at the funeral "no one said more than Elias and at the last his new wife had to put her arms around him to bring an end to all the words" (103). Further, it seems implied that Caldonia makes him overseer after Moses and two other slaves run away (335, 354) because she thinks he is one who will, unlike Moses, promote good will among the slaves and thus prevent further escapes. Elias does not love everyone in the slave community, Moses being an example, but his creation of good will is a central force in the community, an extension of his love for his family and profound emotional attachment to Luke.

While it is understandable that he hates Moses, Elias sees by the end that hating him and trying to take retribution on him is wrong and brings about regrettable consequences. Moses mocks Elias after his failed escape attempt (85), harasses him often (7–9), and causes Celeste to have a miscarriage (326–27). However, when he takes charge as overseer at Caldonia's request after Moses escapes, not to bring good will to the slave community as Caldonia ostensibly thinks, but to show Moses that everything still goes on without him (336–37), and then goes out with Louis to look for Moses (371–74), Elias mistakenly situates himself in a very bad place. He is already legally a powerless slave, but when he and Louis meet the capturers of Moses on the road, he finds himself in the exacerbated position of a powerless slave who has to witness another powerless slave being hobbled by brutal slave patrollers. The patroller Oden Peoples cuts Moses's Achilles tendon to punish him for escaping: "Everyone, except Elias, helped Moses up onto the back of Oden's horse. . . . By rights, Oden could have made Elias the slave carry Moses, but he didn't like the evil that seemed to be building in Elias" (375–76). Elias does silently show his displeasure but does not dare do more because, even though Oden is a Cherokee and not a white man, he is still a slave patroller and above the status of a slave. It would have been better if, no matter what Moses had done, Elias had not let his hatred control him as Celeste had hoped (350–51).

Hating Moses and the consequences of the hatred are bad, but the novel clearly affirms Elias's very positive characterization. During the present time in 1855, Elias never has a surname because he is a slave. However, the surname "Freemen," apparently chosen by his descendants, implies vindication for his mistakes and validates his greatness, the greatness of Celeste never being in question: "The generations of Celeste and Elias Freemen would be legion in Virginia" (351).

It is noteworthy that Augustus frees himself and his family and his lineage ends with his death and that Elias and his family remain in slavery and his lineage continues for generations; this seems somewhat ironic because of the capabilities of the two men and what those capabilities would seem to imply for the future. Augustus can buy himself and his family out of slavery by hiring himself out because he is a skillful "woodcarver whose work people said could bring sinners to tears" (14). (Augustus's son Henry is also a skilled craftsman, a boot maker good enough to make boots for Robbins's family and other white people [112–13].) On the other hand, Elias is only an inept artist who made a comb for Celeste that was "certainly one of the crudest and ugliest instruments in the history of the world" (99). (Walking among the slave cabins with other freeborn black people Dora, her brother Louis, and Caldonia after Henry's death and the escape of three slaves, Fern is probably being condescending when she tells Tessie that a doll Elias made for her, the same doll she remembers on her dying day, is "such a pretty doll" [350].) Yet Augustus, Henry, and Mildred die during the time of slavery, ending their family line,[10] and Elias and his family outlive slavery and continue a living legacy for many generations.

This does not at all imply a criticism of Augustus and his family and black people like them. However, although it would not have been apparent then, it does show that those black people like Elias, who seemed to have the least potential and ability but still persisted in their struggle for freedom, sometimes left a legacy that those like Augustus did not. Augustus and Elias are still equally significant and great as characters, though.

Stamford is a black male slave who seems to have little potential and ability, far less than Elias, but Stamford lives to carry out a legacy of working for the black community and leaves a sign of it, literally, for the world to see. Somewhat in the way Philomena has an obsession with the idea of the city of Richmond that she gets from a slave woman's stories (14–15), Stamford has an obsession with "young stuff" because another slave once told him that having young slave women as sexual partners would help him survive slavery (57, 190). Because he is getting old and still pursuing young women who no longer want him, Stamford is constant trouble (57–58). However, the supernatural experience in the woods after a fight with another slave over a young woman transforms him (193–94, 200–6). The narrator looks ahead twenty years to the time when Elias's son Elwood would meet Stamford in Richmond to become a teacher at Stamford's Richmond Home for Colored Orphans. The Stamford that day twenty years later would be transformed and would think that it "mattered not how long he had wandered in the wilderness, how long they had kept him in chains, how long he had helped them and kept himself in his own chains; none of that mattered now" (353–54). Behind Stamford that day was the corner where more than a hundred years later "they would put that first street sign—STAMFORD AND DELPHIE CROW BLUEBERRY STREET." Stamford would live out a legacy of good work in the black community, which the street sign naming him, his wife, and parts of his transformative supernatural experience would later recognize. Stamford does not achieve what Elias does in terms of loving others and seeking freedom during slavery, and his portrayal is not as positive overall as Elias's and Augustus's. However, in the final analysis his character is positive and, like Elias's, shows that sometimes those slaves with seemingly less ability and potential had the greatest legacies.

In the novel's central freedom quest, Stamford is like Alice in some ways, a more obviously symbolic character defined by "crazy" antics and abrupt change (brought on by a supernatural occurrence in Stamford's case) rather than a realistically portrayed character who struggles for freedom in humanly recognizable ways, like Celeste, Mildred, Augustus, and Elias. While this is true, Stamford and Alice are more obviously symbolic characters who, along with all the other characters and structural elements in the novel, are part of a larger symbol of the black experience, a symbol of everything, a historical whole, a totality that inevitably progresses to freedom.

Three other black male characters—Jebediah Dickson, Louis Cartwright, and Calvin Newman—are largely positive, or at least ambiguously portrayed in the case of Louis. Jebediah's main significance is that, by interacting with Fern Elston, he forces her to a high point of moral development that she never would have attained otherwise. The central thing that we find out about Jebediah is that, although he is apparently a slave, he denies that he is and refuses to act in any way like a slave, refuses to accept anything less than the rights of white people. Beyond the role that he plays in highlighting Fern's development, this relentless insistence on the rights of a free man makes him another more obviously symbolic character, perhaps most comparable to Alice.

Like his sister Dora, there is not much clearly negative about Louis, but unlike his sister, his character is ambiguous because there also is not one thing that is clearly positive about him in the context of the black struggle for freedom. The narrator says that, after their white father William Robbins's stroke, Louis "told [Dora] not to go [to his plantation to take care of him], but [she went because] she had more of her father in her than he did" (362). Understandably, Louis does not love his father, if for nothing else than that he witnessed him abusing their mother in Richmond (118), but Dora witnessed it too and loves him in spite of this. If for no other reason than love is almost always good, Dora's love is good, too; but, though understandable, Louis's dislike, presented in its brief context in the novel, is not clearly good or bad. A free man, Louis is later "surprised at how close" he becomes with Elias (372–73), a slave and one of the novel's exemplars, and suffers emotionally with him and comforts him when the patrollers hobble Moses. Louis even tells the patrollers: "That slave does not belong to you for yall to do with as you please. He is not your property. He is not yours."

Louis's surprise at his closeness to Elias could show that it is superficial, and his words to the patrollers could be just an on-the-spot human response of shock to the anticipated brutality of what is about to happen. However, Louis's feelings also could indicate real change, and maybe, in broader terms than momentary shock, he is genuinely responding to the plight of a slave who he thinks should be free. None of this is clear, though. Also, Louis marries Caldonia after Henry dies, and he, Caldonia, his mother Philomena, and Louis's son Robbins look upon a burning Richmond as the Civil War happens (144–45). Along with the others, he is thus in a sense looking ahead to the freedom that is coming. Although the novel does not tell us, he could be anticipating freedom, wanting it. Perhaps there is an implication that Louis has developed into a free black man who is in favor of freedom for all black people.

Maybe this is true, but his marriage to Caldonia, who is superficial and selfish, and who still had not freed her slaves when they were married at the beginning of the Civil War (383–88), brings this into question. The very last sections of the novel, set at the start of the war, show Louis married to a black woman who never develops beyond her negative character traits, and even more significantly still owns slaves. He is therefore a slave owner himself. In the final analysis, his characterization remains in a gray, ambiguous area, with perhaps some implication that he has truly accepted the idea of freedom for all.

Caldonia's twin brother, Calvin Newman, in spite of coming from the same family as his slave-owning sister and slave-owning mother, empathizes with slaves, supports black freedom, and has a larger vision of freedom generally. Throughout the novel, Calvin always feels differently about slavery. For example, before Henry dies, Calvin has always wanted to free his family's slaves, the "legacy" that his mother so tenaciously defends (66). After Henry dies, he wants to stay among the slaves in the slave cabins as Augustus and Mildred do when they all come to the plantation, but he does not because he is afraid the slaves will not welcome him because he is a free man from a slave-owning family. A photograph of New York that Calvin has symbolizes his larger vision of a free world. In the photograph, there is a dog looking at "a whole world off to the right that the photograph had not captured. Whatever it was might be powerful enough, wonderful enough, to wait until Calvin could arrive and see it and know it for himself" (189–90). This vision of the world is one where all black people can be free. Calvin never makes it to New York, but he does get to Washington (383). At the end, his letter to Caldonia from Washington extolling the free black community there confirms his commitment to the vision of a free world (383–86).

Calvin's vision of freedom develops from his feeling that he is not free. One reason he stays in the oppressive, slaveholding South is to be close to Louis, whom he loves: Once, seeing a pool of water at the base of Louis's neck, "Calvin had wanted to lean over and drink with his tongue from the pool" (189), but "he knew Louis would have tried to kill him right there." His lack of freedom as a gay man is a major reason that he is empathetic to slaves and a supporter of their freedom.[11] (It is ironic that his sister, who apparently has no knowledge of his gayness, is married to and having a child by the man he loves.)

Calvin never has the great courage to reveal that he is gay, never has to persevere and struggle for freedom in slave society as Elias and Augustus do, but among the black men and among all the characters, his portrayal is one of the most positive and sympathetic. This is because he is one of the novel's strongest advocates of a new, free world for all, including black people.

Moses and Henry Townsend are two major black male characters that the novel obviously portrays negatively because they oppress and brutalize slaves, and own, oppress, brutalize, and economically exploit them. Because they are black and mistreat other black people during slavery, perhaps it would seem that their characterizations would be very complex, but actually they are easy to understand when one thinks about the great power of slavery to corrupt *everyone* morally and psychologically, including black people, who maneuvered within its nefarious hierarchy of power.

Moses's characterization is more straightforward. Initially he is a vulnerable but loving, humane slave; Henry giving him the position of overseer is the worst thing that happens to him because he forgets his own vulnerability and becomes mean and inhumane, succumbing to his need to feel important and have power and control over others, a human proclivity of many, no matter what their race or place in society. When Robbins buys Moses for Henry, Moses reveals how vulnerable and also how loving and humane he is when he pleads with Robbins not to separate him and a female slave: "Please, Master Sir . . . we together, her and me. Don't pull us apart. We together. . . . Please, master sir, she and me be family" (172). Robbins ignores Moses's pleas and separates them, buying Moses without buying the woman. After Robbins reprimands Henry for playing around with Moses when Moses is his slave, he gets another strong message about his vulnerability when Henry slaps him once, causing "the pain [to] begin to set in on Moses's face," and then again (124). Nevertheless, when he gets the "power" over other black people as overseer, he is always mean and sometimes does terribly abusive things like mocking Elias after his failed escape (85), pushing Alice "down as hard as he could" so that she starts crying (271), slapping his wife Priscilla to her knees (263), and making pregnant Celeste work in the fields and have a miscarriage (326–27). Moses goes so far as to try to take the place of the master when Henry dies, and runs away when Caldonia rebuffs him (329–30, 334–36). It is not clear that he knows he has let slavery victimize him by turning him into a mean, inhumane person in his quest for power and importance. However, before the slave patrollers hobble him, he probably realizes his vulnerability again: He says, "Please, yall, don't hurt me like that. Please" (373).

Henry's characterization is a little more complex, but not much. He is a victim of corruption by the idea of the power and privilege of owning slaves when he is young during his formative years, and thus does not understand that it is bad. Essentially, he spends most of his time from the age of nine, when his father, Augustus, buys his mother, Mildred (15–16), to the age of nineteen or twenty, when Augustus finally buys him (21, 44–46), under the influence of one of the two richest white aristocratic slave owning men in Manchester County, William Robbins (377). He becomes Robbins's groom, "prove[s] himself to Robbins" (20), and becomes a practical, almost indispensable part of Robbins's life; Robbins thus treats him kindly and he lives a fairly comfortable life. Therefore, he fails to see anything wrong with Robbins and his life as an aristocratic slaveholder. In fact, he ends up respecting Robbins and greatly respecting the slave-owning life, and becomes a slave owner himself.[12]

Henry reveals his corruption several times by his vision of slavery and failure to understand its immorality. The first indication is his insensitivity to his parents and failure to show up to meet them sometimes when they come to visit on Sundays before Augustus buys him (17–19). Another is his revelation to Augustus, just after he becomes free, that he is not feeling any different now that he is free: Henry "wanted to know if he was supposed to [feel any different], but he did not know how to ask that. He wondered who was waiting now for Robbins to come riding up on Sir Guilderham" (49). Waiting for Robbins was his job as Robbins's groom, the position in which he felt Robbins's positive attention and got a vision of the power of the slave owner that made him blind to slavery's immorality.

Later, Henry shows the full effects of his immoral indoctrination when he buys his first slave, Moses, with Robbins's help. When Augustus and Mildred respond in utter shock and disbelief, Henry says that he has done nothing wrong, nothing a white man would not have done: "I ain't broke no law" (138). Because of his years with and influence by Robbins, whom he sees as a great white man who represents what is lawful and right, he cannot distinguish between true morality and a white man's power to create and use the law immorally. He lacks any moral feeling or understanding and has no sense of the striking contradiction in his ownership of slaves, no sense of the idea that, as Mildred thinks, "thou shall own no one, havin been owned once your own self" (137). Later, Henry did say he wanted to be a different, supposedly more humane kind of slave master, but "did not understand that the kind of world he wanted to create was doomed before he had even spoken the first syllable of the word *master*" (64). So this is not a serious sentiment because the idea of being a different kind of master is specious in the first place. Henry never has any moral feeling or understanding and fools himself into thinking that he does.

Among the black men, several obviously play major roles in the novel's central task of working toward freedom, but black women such as Celeste, Mildred, and Alice make more valuable contributions. Black men such as Augustus and Elias are stalwarts in the freedom struggle, too, and black women such as Caldonia and Maude are oppressors. However, black women generally stand out more for their positive characterizations.

White Male Characters in *The Known World*

Although Barnum Kinsey's portrayal is brief, it is the most positive among the white people in the novel; although Barnum is incapable of the analysis that would lead to an understanding of the immorality of racism and of racist law that enforces slavery, he thinks, feels, and acts toward black people in a way that shows that he could accept black freedom, which separates him from all the other white characters. Barnum's thinking and action are ironic because he is the poorest white man in the county (209–10), and thus in slavery's hierarchy only differentiated from black people by the myth of his whiteness, and because he is also a racist who does not want anyone to think that he is "on the nigger side" (303). Nevertheless, when the slave patrollers accost Augustus and then sell him illegally, he protests to the buyers that "Augustus Townsend is a free man. You can't buy him. Just leave him be" (214). Later, he informs Sheriff John Skiffington about what the patrollers did, telling him that Augustus "was a free and clear man, and the law said so. Augustus never hurt me, never said bad to me. . . . I regret what happened to Augustus" (303). He is a racist who can only see that selling Augustus back into slavery was wrong because he was legally free, not because slavery is wrong, but at the same time the fact that he can feel for Augustus as a human being implies an unconscious sense of human equality. The same empathy that implies the potential for equality is apparent when he tries to stop the patrollers from hobbling Moses because they hold him responsible for the sheriff's death: "He ain't the one that hurt John. . . . And besides, it look like he done learned his lesson" because he is pleading with the men not to hurt him (373). Barnum believes that as a white man and slave patroller he has a duty to uphold slavery. However, unlike the other two patrollers and seemingly most other white people in the South as depicted in the novel, he never hates black people and has genuine feeling and respect for basic human rights. His outstanding difference is that his attitude has implications for a different, free world.[13]

Sheriff John Skiffington is a vastly inferior human being to Kinsey, the socially low slave patroller under his command; in spite of his pretentions, Skiffington is one of the most negatively portrayed white people. Skiffington, who creates a self-image and persona to play his role and profit in slave society, rationalizes his actions, obfuscates the truth, disingenuously perceives the world and his relationships, and unconsciously harbors a virulent, ultimately deadly hatred of black people necessary to maintain the institution of slavery. More generally, he is a morally confused hypocrite whose characterization is subtle, complex, and ambiguous because of his labyrinthine deviousness.

Skiffington's relationship with Minerva and the white community combines rationalization, disingenuousness, and obfuscation. He pretends to be against slavery because he is a Christian and consequently above owning slaves (29–30). Part of what he tells himself about his reason for keeping Minerva as a slave is that he does not want to risk selling her into a harsh slave life, but it is easy to see that he does not sell her because he wants to get along with the white people in Manchester County and keep his job (33–34). So he and Winifred pretend that Minerva is a family member and not really a slave while not saying anything publicly against slavery (166). They tell each other that they do not support slavery while not saying publicly that they believe Minerva is a family member.

Skiffington rationalizes and obfuscates when he tells himself that he does not act on his sexual attraction to Minerva because he is a man of God. He "knew many a white man who had taken black women as their own, and among those men, he would have been thought normal. But he saw himself living in the company of God, who had married him to Winifred, and he believed God would abandon him if he took Minerva. And Winifred would discover what he had done, even if Minerva never said a word" (307–8). The true reasons for his not taking action on his desires are not that he lives "in the company of God," as "he saw himself," or "God would abandon him," as "he believed." More likely, one of the reasons he fears a relationship with Minerva is that, if the relationship were discovered, it would ruin his self-righteous image as a white man who did not take black women. Although it is not clear why he thinks Winifred would find out if Minerva did not say anything, the other reason is that Winifred, not God, would abandon him if she found out. Despite the ambiguity caused by his moral confusion, Skiffington definitely uses Christianity to hide the truth.

The sale of Moses to William Robbins in his jail reveals Skiffington obfuscating the truth to keep his job. When Robbins threatens to buy Moses just to shoot him if he says another word, Skiffington thinks but does not say: "*I arrest you for the murder of this nigger right in front of my eyes*" (172). Skiffington hides behind the delusion that he would arrest Robbins because he sees himself as a Christian who believes that the murder of any human being, even a slave, is wrong. If his belief truly had substance, first of all he would speak, and Robbins would not have made him sheriff and he would not be in this situation where Robbins is buying the slave Moses in his jail. Robbins is powerful, and he might lose his job as sheriff if he speaks. This is the truth beneath his obfuscation.

When Augustus disappears, Skiffington uses an ideal conceptualization of the law to hide the truth about his selfishly motivated inaction. He tells Mildred that the "law always cares" about what happened to Augustus (307). Also, when his deputy, Counsel Skiffington, does not report that Mildred and others came to him about Augustus' disappearance, because "they were three niggers talking about another nigger" (309–10), Skiffington tells him that everyone is important in the eyes of the law (309–10). However, Skiffington undercuts his implication that he really represents this ideal of the law and will take action. Hiding behind the words of Genesis 50:17, "*forgive the trespass of the servants of God of thy father*" (310), he fails to punish the slave patrollers who sold Augustus, finally saying to them, "I don't want to hear anything like this about yall again." (In comparison to Barnum Kinsey, who has the courage to speak on behalf of Augustus, Skiffington never truly stands up for Augustus.) He talks about the law and thinks about the Bible, but he is only hiding the fact that he does not want to take action that will jeopardize his place as the sheriff who upholds the slave system.

His killing of Mildred reveals his deadly hatred of black people, which is essential for a sheriff enforcing slavery's laws. At first, when he demands that Mildred "surrender the property [Moses]" (364), he cannot remember her name, remember if he has ever spoken it, or remember her husband Augustus's name. After accidentally shooting Mildred, Skiffington says, "What have I asked except civility and righteousness? . . . I asked nothing of that nigger, except what is proper and right. Not more than that do I ask of any nigger. No More" (366). The problem with remembering Mildred's name could be a result of the stress of the situation. However, after he has called a slave "property," not remembering her and Augustus's names more likely implies his denial of their reality as free human beings. For him, underneath everything, black people are slaves and "property," and he hates them and refuses to acknowledge them when they are free people who can give themselves first and last names, "Mildred Townsend" and "Augustus Townsend."[14] After shooting Mildred, he talks about "civility," "righteousness," and "what is proper and right," still trying to cloak himself in the law and Christianity. However, his words have the implication, behind his words and the entire scene, that he hates black people, and this hatred has always been right below the surface of his consciousness.

Also very negatively portrayed, the aristocratic William Robbins is unabashedly brutal in dealing with slaves and is in many ways different from Skiffington, but somewhat like him in that his ideological commitment to slavery is a source of confusion that leads to contradictory actions. Robbins's confusion and contradictory actions center on two people, his mistress Philomena and Henry Townsend. The problem is that he believes in the inferiority of and hates slaves because of the ideology of the slave system and is supposed to feel the same way about Philomena and Henry, but surprisingly he feels the human emotion of love for Philomena and genuine fondness for Henry. As the time approached when Augustus would finish paying for and take Henry from Robbins, he "was surprised to know that he would miss the boy. He had not been so surprised about his feelings for a black human being since realizing that he loved Philomena" (112). In spite of his general hatred for slaves, he actually has feelings of love and fondness for two black people who were slaves and that he has gotten to know well. His human feelings explain his bond to Philomena and simultaneous abuse of her and seemingly strange actions of making Henry, his own ex-slave, his protégé, setting him up as a slave owner, and supporting him.

One scene in the novel specifies what underlies Robbins's perplexing relationship to Henry. When Philomena runs away to Richmond with his black children, Robbins goes to get her and takes Henry, whom he already likes because as his groom Henry has curried his favor throughout the years (20–21, 112). In Richmond, Robbins has a realization that augments his feelings for Henry. Henry comforts his frightened, distraught children when he fights with Philomena. "Dora and Louis were in the bed and the girl was holding her brother," but after Henry sings and creates a diversion, "Dora was able to let go of her brother" (118–19). Robbins realizes then that "the world would not be very good to the children he had had with Philomena, but whatever world it would be, he wanted Henry in it for them" (121). Thus he helps and supports Henry.

Robbins never untangles his confused thinking because of his commitment to slavery's ideology, never understands his confusion because he loves a black woman whom he is not supposed to love, probably never comes to terms with loving his black children whom he is not supposed to love or acknowledge,[15] and probably never understands his fondness for Henry. Henry's importance does get through to him though, and this explains much about their relationship and Robbins's characterization. Maybe Robbins is confused because he believes in black inferiority but is trying to help a black person he likes, and this might be the reason for the following strange-sounding advice to Henry: "There are white men out there, Henry, who ain't got nothin. You might as well step in and take what they ain't takin. Why not? God is in his heaven and he don't care most of the time. The trick of life is to know when God does care and do all you need to do behind his back" (140–41).

One other white male character, John Skiffington's cousin Counsel Skiffington, is a virulent racist and one of the most horrific people in the novel; his characterization as an embodiment of the horror of slavery is easy to understand. His journey through several southern states, after smallpox hits his North Carolina plantation and he burns it, is more of a surreal, dreamlike psychological journey in the mind of a racist slave owner than a literal journey (223–33), and if one reads the journey as a representation of the racist mind, it is easy to understand. Aspects of Counsel's characterization are surreal and dreamlike to illustrate points about racist white thinking, points that are clear in spite of the form of their presentation. Counsel himself is largely a straightforwardly racist white man; his portrayal has much less subtlety, nuance, and complexity than John Skiffington and Barnum Kinsey's, and less than William Robbins's too.

Other Characters—Black, White, Native American, Female, Male

The novel's secondary characters also deserve a brief discussion. Among the house slaves, Caldonia's personal maid, Loretta; Zeddie, the cook; and Zeddie's husband, Bennett, are complementary characters living in the house taking care of Henry and Caldonia and then Caldonia alone after Henry dies. Their lives are deemed more privileged than those of field slaves. Loretta puts a knife to Moses's throat to defend Caldonia against him when he demands his freedom (330), and this is probably what stands out most among the actions of these characters.

Field slaves Tessie, Elwood, Gloria, and Delphie help to carry out the plot, too. It is significant that Celeste and Elias's daughter Tessie survives slavery to be ninety-seven years old (67, 350) and carry on the legacy of her parents, the "Freemen" legacy (351). Their son Elwood also carries on the family legacy after slavery by teaching at Stamford's Richmond Home for Colored Orphans (353–54). Delphie outlives slavery to become Stamford's wife and unite with him in the work he does to help black people; more than a hundred years after slavery, the city names a Richmond street after her and Stamford: "STAMFORD AND DELPHIE CROW BLUEBERRY STREET." Gloria's role is more purely complementary: She is the young woman over whom Stamford gets in a fight, thus starting a chain of events leading to his transformation (190–207), and she runs away with another slave, her new boyfriend, as Moses's escape is distracting everyone (335, 339).

Stennis, the slave of the white kidnapper Darcy who buys Augustus and sells him back into slavery, and his master are both total degenerates who reflect the reality of slavery's ruthless exploitation of black people and degradation of all people. All of their interactions confirm this.

Among the free black people, Ramsey Elston and Valtims Moffett stand out somewhat. Ramsey stands out only because of what his wife, Fern Elston, does in response to him; she progresses as a human being at least partly by forcing herself reluctantly to come to terms with Ramsey's negative character traits compared to the positive ones of Jebediah Dickson, a slave who is supposed to be inferior to a free man like Ramsey. Valtims is the free black preacher and a slave owner himself who plays the well-known role of the minister who tells slaves to obey their masters (82–83, 87). He is another black character debased by the nefarious system of slavery.

Harvey Travis and Oden Peoples, slave patrollers as well as, respectively, a poor white and a poor Cherokee, show how the hierarchy of slavery corrupted poor white people and other poor nonwhites. Slavery makes both of these characters ruthless and brutal in dealing with slaves because they want some recognition and to feel that they have some power in a system that gives them very little power, sometimes less than free black people.

CHAPTER 4

The Stories of *Lost in the City*

The stories in *Lost in the City* (1992) stand alone individually, which is also true of the stories in Jones's second short-story collection, *All Aunt Hagar's Children* (2006), but the stories in each volume also collectively create a thematic whole. Further, the corresponding stories among the fourteen in each volume have direct connections, and the two volumes together form a larger thematic whole.

Among the fourteen stories in *Lost in the City*, twelve are told by a third-person omniscient narrator who has some of the very distinctive characteristics of the omniscient narrator in Jones's novel, *The Known World*. Although the stories are somewhat disjointed and fragmented, the narrator creates a more unified, contiguous plot structure than in the highly fragmented, disjointed, long novel. Also, obviously the narrator does not talk about as many characters in the short stories as in the novel. Further, the narrator in the twelve third-person-omniscient stories for the most part does not create the same kind of unique irony and wry humor that is so prevalent in the novel. However, many of the characters' lines and many of the narrator's own lines are laugh-out-loud funny, as in the novel. The omniscient narrator again often moves godlike back and forth through the past, present, and future, presenting plot events and commenting on characters' lives. Reminiscent of Jones saying that he is the "'god' of the people in [*The Known World*], [who] could see their first days [analeptic vision] and their last days [proleptic vision] and all that was in between" (*The Known World* interview, P.S. 4),[1] the narrator in the stories implies a godlike vision but narrates only selectively. Because of the omniscient narrator's vision and because the two volumes constitute a thematic whole, the short stories are symbolic of everything, a historical whole, a totality of black experience in many of the same ways that the novel is.

The characters in *Lost in the City* are "lost" and in danger, and connecting to black community and various aspects of black culture and tradition is central. The godlike third-person narrator reveals the importance of the characters' abilities to establish pathways back and forth that are psychological—and sometimes seemingly spiritual, sometimes seemingly psychic or supernatural—that connect people, communities, and general tradition[2] in the South and North through memories, stories, letters, specific cultural traditions, photographs, songs, and history. That is, the characters largely stay in the North, "lost" in Washington, D.C., but consciously and subconsciously they move back and forth over the journey between the South and the North that they and other black people have taken. The more direct thematic revelations of the godlike narrator in twelve stories will obviously be somewhat different from the perspective of the limited first-person narrator in two stories. At the same time however, among the stories collectively, the omniscient narrator in the third-person stories sets the dominant thematic direction. As in *The Known World,* the omniscient narrator sometimes chooses to be cryptic, particularly in revealing the reality of something that is seemingly spiritual, psychic, or supernatural, and here as in the novel the narrator's use of the cryptic makes the writing compelling.

Although it does not happen in every story, the establishment of this psychic, supernatural, spiritual back-and-forth road between the South and North in which memories, stories, letters, specific cultural traditions, photographs, songs, and history connect people, family, community, and broader tradition is clearly the key to black sustenance and ongoing survival.[3] In five stories—"Lost in the City," "Gospel," "His Mother's House," "The Sunday Following Mother's Day," and "An Orange Line Train to Ballston"—in the specific context of the individual story, there is no clear connection to family, community, and tradition, or the connection is ambiguous or questionable. The connection is ambiguous and questionable, but there is perhaps more potential for connection, in three stories: "The First Day," "The Night Rhonda Ferguson Was Killed," and "Young Lions." Two stories—"A Butterfly on F Street" and "A Dark Night"—are hard to classify or categorize in these terms. The clear potential for connection is portrayed in three stories: "The Store," "A New Man," and "Marie."

Through its very general theme that black people must come to terms with their own lives and stories as parts of black communities, "The Girl Who Raised Pigeons" lays the foundation for the other stories in the volume. The story's main focus is Betsy Ann Morgan's life between the ages of five and about twelve, but more broadly it portrays her life as a part of her community from the time of her conception to the end when she is around twelve.

In the first two paragraphs the narrator references pigeons in the context of the sleep, dream, and memory of Betsy Ann and her father, Robert Morgan. The narrator asserts for Betsy Ann a perception of reality that is beyond the normal, and perhaps supernatural. Betsy Ann is unaware of this supernatural-like region of her perception, and the narrator does not explain it, but this is what generates her desire to raise pigeons. Young Betsy Ann is the predecessor in a line of mostly older characters in later stories who have defining memories and perceptions of their lives, often their past lives, that are sometimes conscious, but more significantly are subconscious.[4] Sometimes the subconscious of the characters becomes clearly conscious, but even if it does not, the characters unknowingly access the subconscious, or the narrator reveals how it influences them.

The ambiguity about Betsy Ann's attraction to pigeons notwithstanding, the pigeons clearly stand out as a symbol of flight and movement back and forth that relates to the black community. The characters have beliefs about pigeons, like Robert's belief that nobody likes the birds (3) and Miss Jenny's belief that they carry diseases (4), but none of this is true in the story. What is true is that, after the community barber Miles Patterson gives two pigeons to Betsy at her request, the pigeons at first fly back to Miles's house every day, but then, after making a nest at Betsy's, they return to her every day after flying away. ("In the Blink of God's Eye," the first story in *All Aunt Hagar's Children*, will provide further insight into who Miles Patterson is, and also insight into "The Girl Who Raised Pigeons.") The pigeons stay and reproduce until the "spring and summer of 1961 when the Myrtle Street [black community] emptied of people" (21). Apparently, this is a reference to a rumored communal breakdown that is the result of encroachment by the white power structure: The "railroad people were planning to take all the land around Myrtle Street, perhaps up to L Street and down to H Street" (15). After people start to leave the black community following its breakdown, rats cross the roof of a vacant house next to Robert's and kill all but two pigeons; the remaining two who are unhurt fly away. One of the two birds who had not been hurt would return for about an hour sometimes, but then on "what turned out to be the last day" (24), he flew away. The story ends, "She did nothing, aside from following him, with her eyes, with her heart, as far as she could" (25). As a symbol of back-and-forth movement relating to the black community, the pigeon flying away seems ominous because it is leaving Betsy and the community, which is no longer supportive, for good. However, older characters in later stories will provide a broader context to look at black community and how black people move back and forth physically, psychically, and spiritually in the community extending from the South to the North.

In "The Girl Who Raised Pigeons," Betsy Ann is too young to know the past, to know about the journey to the North, and to be able to move in memory and consciousness back and forth between the southern past and the northern present. However, the narrator shows that the need to draw sustenance from this knowledge of the past and back-and-forth movement is somehow a part of her, which explains her attraction to the pigeons. As it will become clear as the stories progress, the pigeons' flights to old and new homes symbolize black journeys. The destruction of the pigeons, their flight away, the encroachment on the black community by the white, and Betsy's sadness at the end all suggest the plight of black life; however, at the end, Betsy does follow the last pigeon with her eyes and heart. There is a suggestion of endurance and transcendence of great difficulty here, too, and this will turn out to be a dominant theme throughout the stories.[5]

The stories that most clearly depict the lack of connection portrayed in the "The Girl Who Raised Pigeons" are "Lost in the City," "Gospel," "His Mother's House," "The Sunday Following Mother's Day," and "An Orange Line Train to Ballston." Lydia Walsh in "Lost in the City" is the most disconnected, "lost" character in the volume. A lawyer with a degree from Yale, Lydia has been to a lot of places around the world and has recorded her story in a diary and in pictures, but after her mother dies, she finds that she has nothing to connect and sustain her. In her confusion, she pays a cab driver to "get [her] lost in the city" (148). As she goes through the streets where she grew up in Washington, her confusion does not decrease. Nothing from her past as she knows it grounds her in the present. In spite of her education and the places she has been, the stories she has recorded, and her revisiting the places of her younger years, she has no good prospects of grounding herself in a meaningful tradition. The last two paragraphs, particularly the last one, recalling a conversation with her mother, suggest an inkling of her recognition of a past tradition that is meaningful, but this is tenuous at best.[6]

Vivian L. Slater in "Gospel" is much different from Lydia, but her predicament is scarcely better: Vivian sings, but the real gospel is her own deluded self-truth that she has to confront, the deception of which leaves her shocked and confused. The story centers on how Vivian, fifty-seven years old, maintains her vision of her own superiority by focusing on the supposed inferiority of her "best friend" (184) Diane McCollough, also fifty-seven. "Diane lived in a house half the size of Vivian's on 9th Street Southeast, not far from Lincoln Park. . . . Diane lived with her second husband, Harry, and her youngest daughter from her first marriage, along with her daughter's only child, an overweight boy of four who had been spoiled beyond redemption. Two of Diane's sons were in Lorton for selling cocaine" (185). In a backhanded defense of Diane for interacting in her daughter's troubled marriage, Vivian would say, "And think of that poor ugly daughter of hers." The shock and confusion occur at the end, when Vivian witnesses Diane having a love tryst with a man, making her see Diane from an entirely different perspective: Diane was a "woman who had lost her heart, a woman she did not know, had never met in her life" (198).

In turn, this new perspective forces Vivian to look more closely at the reality of her own life. She has not told anyone, but her husband, Ralph, is dying. Waiting for her at home, he "might have peed on himself again" (200). Further, in "a cheap metal box" at home, "she kept the licenses from her three marriages, along with the divorce documents. And from the first common-law marriage, she kept a letter, in childlike block letters and misspelled words, that the man had written to her from two thousand miles away, promising that they would be one forever." She must realize that her life is not better than the life of Diane that she had imagined earlier, and she must suspect that she is not as good as the transformed Diane, "a woman she did not know." However, she still does not think that God "should waste [men like the one she saw] upon women like Diane McCollough."

So at the end Vivian sees the world and herself differently, but she is still confused, as shown by the last paragraph: sitting in her car, she can only see shadows through the snow-covered windows, cannot clearly hear what people are saying outside, and cannot read her watch. She is not free of the "gospel," her own superficial "tradition" of self-truth.

"His Mother's House" portrays characters separated from tradition in one of the most extreme cases of familial and human fracturing in *Lost in the City.* Something in Joyce Moses's life has caused her to develop an image of self-inadequacy. Maybe it is her experience with men, which the narrator explains in talking about her desire to hang onto her boyfriend Rickey Madison: "He was the first man in her life who had never beaten her. And for a long time she thought that because he did not beat her, he did not care for her as much and that one morning she would wake up and, like the others, he would be gone" (158). Having a man, even an abusive man, makes her feel worthwhile, and since he makes her feel worthwhile, has stayed with her, and does not beat her, she is desperate to keep Rickey. Because he describes himself as "a family man without a family" (173) when she first meets him, she promises to give him children. However, she has had a tubal ligation and cannot have any more children. In spite of Rickey's later participation in dope dealing, his desire for a family is positive, but the fracturing of their relationship and larger fracturing of their family would ensue with Rickey's inevitable discovery of Joyce's desperate, great lie. Beyond this, the characters in the story are so strung out on the riches of dope money, or actually on dope, that knowledge of potential access to any saving tradition is hidden from them in some murky region between the subconscious and the unconscious.[7]

The main symbol of tradition is Joyce's "whole life, in dozens of pictures . . . seen through the glass top of [an] old coffee table" (151). The separation from the pictures by the glass is symbolic, but as time goes on and the table runs out of space, the symbol becomes more clearly one of fracture. "In some cases, a face was hidden by the picture above it or next to it; in others, there were missing limbs, and in still others, entire bodies were gone, except for a sleeve or shoe here and there" (169). Joyce tells her son Santiago, the dope dealer, that the pictures represent her life (151), but she is scarcely aware of the symbolism of the pictures' separation by glass, and certainly not aware of the fracturing symbolism of the second description of the pictures.

The plot plays out when everything breaks apart at the end; it becomes clear that the new, expensive house Santiago has bought Joyce with dope money is only a home for fractured dreams. Her son Santiago murders her godson Humphrey, who is Santiago's dealer and who calls her "Mama Joyce." Rickey, who has become a driver and bodyguard for Santiago, witnesses the murder and runs away when Joyce "began to scream his name" (174). (He runs away before discovering the tubal ligation, but still runs away.) Santiago jumps in his Range Rover and runs away, too. Santiago has an apartment but recently has been staying with Joyce's mother, who rejects the drug life and lives in "Judiciary House, an H Street apartment Building for senior citizens and the disabled" (171). (The mother's appearance is brief, but she seems to be one of the more securely grounded characters.) Although he bought Joyce's house, this choice by Santiago to live in the grandmother's "poor" house obviously is implicitly a negative comment on Joyce's house, which Joyce apparently does not understand, but Santiago must subliminally. At the end, Joyce unlocks all her doors so that Santiago can get into her house because "outside that house there was a very cruel world and she did not like to think that her child was out there without a place to come to" (175). Ironically, in the context of Joyce's thinking, he will never have a home, with all of its connotations of a sustaining place, in his mother's house, and neither will anyone else. (In spite of the negative elements, this story adds to the diversity of the volume, and it is one of Jones's best because of the power of its portrayal.)

Portraying Madeline Williams trying to find ways to come to terms with the sudden, inexplicable stabbing of her mother by her father, Samuel, when she is four and her brother, Sam, is ten, "The Sunday Following Mother's Day" alludes to the importance of connecting pathways and journeys that support and sustain Madeline and her family after their tragedy. However, she never finds connection, and there is no evidence that she will.

Madeline shows potential to connect, though. She goes to Columbia University, but her educational journey is not meaningful symbolically. However, she does continually ask, "Why did he do it?" (126). Sam grows up to travel throughout the world, but his journeys are not meaningful symbolical connections, as his implicit rejection of past tradition shows. He tells his wife: "We're never gonna believe in anything but right now. . . . Maybe a little of the tomorrow mornin but no farther than that" (130).

The answer to why he did it opens up potential symbolic connecting and sustaining pathways through stories, but Madeline finds no story to answer the question. She asks her namesake Aunt Maddie why he did it, makes tapes about the conversations with Maddie, and talks to other people who might know. Maddie has no story to answer her question, and none emerges elsewhere. From jail at Lorton, however, Samuel does try to tell a story that will connect him with his daughter. He writes "in the most beautiful handwriting of anyone she had ever seen" (128), but he "spoke of everything in the world except the Why, and over time she lost the courage to ask" (128–29). However, his actions when he gets out of jail are still in essence an attempt to construct connecting, sustaining "narratives." By then, he is an almost toothless, bedraggled old man, but he unexpectedly shows up at Madeline's apartment on the Sunday after Mother's Day. He drives her to the home where she has put her retarded son. On this trip, Samuel shows his grandson a level of humane treatment that Madeline has never shown him. This does not mean that he understands why he killed her mother, or that his "narrative" is the source of connection that she needs. Still, however, the "narrative" of his actions of humanity toward her son could be meaningful. Madeline completely misses the message that his actions could convey, though, and at the end she angrily watches Samuel in her apartment parking lot trying to fix his broken-down old car. This is an indication of another failed journey, a well-intended one that has literally broken down in this case.

In spite of her education at Columbia, Madeline never does understand how to make the connection she needs to make. The very well-educated Madeline is almost as "lost" as the similarly educated Lydia in "Lost in the City." "Root Worker," the corresponding story in *All Aunt Hagar's Children,* shows Madeline years later going back to her home in Person County, North Carolina, with others from Washington and then returning to Washington. After they return, a character tells a story that solves a mystery of evil conjuring. This does not mean that her brother killed his wife earlier because of conjuring, but the folk story from the South that solves the mystery connects and sustains symbolically. Also, the trip back to North Carolina and then back to Washington again makes the point about the back-and-forth of tradition. However, Madeline is still "lost" in the specific context of "The Sunday Following Mother's Day."

Marvella "Velle" Watkins in "An Orange Line Train to Ballston" lives among symbolic pathways but, because she sees her life as "blocks of time" (108, 115), she seems incapable of opening herself up to pathways to find what she wants. The symbolic pathways are orange and blue Washington, D.C., subway lines, both of which will take Marvella where she needs to go in the city; on these lines, Marvella is in search of a dreadlocked black man whom she wants to ask her out, seemingly because he appeals to something deep and ineffable in her. She first sees him on the orange line. However, during the course of the story, she sees him on both lines: "Over the next several weeks she saw the dreadlock man only four or five times, and on most mornings she simply took whatever train came first [orange or blue]" (113). Before this, however, she has said to herself that maybe "he only went on the orange line" (113), and she convinces herself that this must be true. It finally turns out that she will only look for him on an orange-line train: She "would take herself and [her children] off to the subway determined to wait for him, for an orange line train." One day she severely reprimands her son after they get on the orange-line train and he asks her "why they had to all the time wait when the blue train was like the orange" (114). After that she does not see the dreadlocked man again, and does "not look for him anymore. But for some time, as she went about her days with their blocks of time, she would find herself comparing his hair with other dreadlocks she saw. By then the subway people had extended the orange line all the way to Vienna" (115).

Marvella is just as "lost" as the characters in the last four stories discussed, but the consequences for her are perhaps not as dire. It does seem, though, that she needs to find the dreadlocked man because he somehow represents an important connection, as shown when he catches her daughter on the subway when she almost falls, "almost as if it had been planned, as if he had known two stops or so back that the child would begin to fall at that moment" (108). Marvella sees her life in limiting "blocks of time" and lacks vision and imagination, and apparently she will never find the man or connect to anything in a meaningful way. Although it is not clear if this will have serious consequences, it is still not good.

In "The First Day," "The Night Rhonda Ferguson Was Killed," and "Young Lions," the connection to a meaningful tradition is ambiguous and questionable, but the potential for it seems greater than in the five stories discussed above. The perception of this does not primarily come from the fact that the main characters are all young people who can change positively, but youth does contribute to the perception. This is probably most true in "The First Day," one of the volume's two first-person stories and one of the two shortest.

Because "The First Day" is so short and the main character, a five-year-old girl, is so young, any conclusions about a connection to tradition are tentative but, also because she is young, she has the potential to find this connection. Her illiterate mother takes her to school for the first day and has to ask another girl's mother to fill out the enrollment forms for her. After meeting her teacher and giving the girl instructions for the day, the mother has "quivering [lips]" (31) as she kneels in the hall beside the girl before leaving, and then she stands and walks away with loud footsteps.[8] At the end, the voices of the other schoolchildren sound like "all the children in the world, [but] I can still hear my mother's footsteps above it all" (31).

The girl's observation of the illiterate mother may reveal a positive story about the mother that can be the beginning of the girl's own story, the symbol of a connecting pathway to a life of survival, a foundation of the black tradition that stands in opposition to oppression. The daughter witnesses the mother's strength and love when she sacrifices her pride by revealing her illiteracy to get the forms filled out. Also, the mother's quivering lips as she kneels beside her daughter and her walking loudly out tell a story of love and determination. The sound of the mother walking in the last sentence symbolizes the mother's story on which the girl can build her story, her own symbolic pathway to move forward with strength, love, and determination as a black woman.

The primary characters in "The Night Rhonda Ferguson Was Killed" are a group of black high-school girls who, except for one, are highly trouble prone, adrift, and unconsciously searching for what will give them stability and wholeness; what they find by the end is a black song that is tantamount to a story that potentially can stabilize them and connect them positively to black home and community, closely related traditional bulwarks. Literal and figurative journeys take place. Throughout most of the story, the characters are riding tumultuously, with a lot of arguing and animosity, through the streets of Washington in a car driven by a high-school girl named Cassandra G. Lewis. An "orphan set adrift in the world" (38), Cassandra is most obviously the one who is unconsciously looking for connection to home and community, among the girls in the car, among black people in the streets through which they are passing. She thinks her friend Rhonda Ferguson, a very talented singer, will give her a job when she signs her record contract, and she will go off with Rhonda to make a lot of money, which is the journey that she wants to make.

As it turns out, though, Rhonda's boyfriend kills her and throws Cassandra's world into turmoil, and it is another girl, named Anita Hughes, the one less adrift and trouble prone, who at the end sings a song that brings her some peace and potentially puts the world in a positive perspective. At Anita's house after the murder, Cassandra talks: "'I got to be goin. . . . I got to be goin home,' Cassandra whispered, saying *home* as if it were a foreign word" (53). Instead of letting her leave, Anita's mother puts Cassandra in bed and makes her daughter a pallet by it. "Sometime way late in the night, Cassandra spoke out. . . . She asked Anita to sing that song she had sung in the car on the way home. Anita sang; long after her parents had gone to bed, long after she stopped wondering if Cassandra was listening, Anita sang. She sang on into the night for herself alone, her voice pushing back everything she did not yet understand" (54).

The song is like a story that one identifies with; it represents the home and community that Cassandra is looking for. (The other girls have heard the song in the car, and it has the same meaning for them.) Cassandra needs to take the figurative journey to home and community through the song. Cassandra does not understand this, and Anita does "not yet understand," either, but nonetheless it is true. The girls in "Night Rhonda Ferguson" are, with the exception of Anita, perhaps headed toward lives of crime, but because they are young and because of what happens at the end, the potential is also there for them to connect to home and community.

In "Rhonda Ferguson," as is often true in *Lost in the City,* the adept humor created by the omniscient narrator adds to the experience of reading the story. There is also a significant range of characters, topics, settings, and experiences in the volume. "Young Lions," the story following "Rhonda Ferguson," displays this range by going beyond the preceding story into the world of criminality.

Only seventeen when his father, "slaving away [his] life to raise him," puts him out of the house because of his associations with criminal-type people (68–70), Caesar Matthews in "Young Lions" needs to find a pathway from criminality back to the traditional bulwarks of home and community before moving forward in a positive present. The end suggests a pathway that Caesar is on in the present, one that he needs to take into the past to recover the saving story, and another one forward again into a positive present; concomitantly, it suggests a story or a memory of the home and community of his past that he needs to recall to bring to the present for his survival.

After putting his gun in his girlfriend's face following an altercation after they pull off a criminal scam, Caesar is confused: There "was something in the air, but he could not make out what it was" (76). He keeps looking behind him, expecting to see something or somebody as he confusedly walks forward: "He continued looking behind him as he made his way up 17th Street. He took out [his] address book, but found he could not read the names or the numbers under the feeble street lights." He ran and "kept trying to read the names and numbers. . . . He did not know what was in the air. He only knew that tonight would not be a night to be without shelter." Besides the implication of 17th Street being a confusing pathway on a confusing journey, there is the implication of an important but unreadable story in the phone book and generally an irretrievable memory of something that is dangerous to forget. He feels in jeopardy in the night reality, which is ironic for a "young lion."

"Something in the air" is a pathway to go back to read and remember the story of home and community and to come back again to a present in which he can then survive. ("Something in the air" is also like the sound of the walking at the end of "The First Day" and the sound of the song at the end of "Rhonda Ferguson." They all are symbols or suggestions of pathways or directions that can carry the characters somewhere they need to go, but of which they are unconscious.) Caesar looks back in an unconscious, confused, symbolic attempt to read and remember his past story of home and community, and moves forward in confusion literally unable to read the story of his present in his address book. While he is confused, and already twenty-four years old (57), potentially the back-and-forth attempt to read and remember the past story and read the present story can still lead to comprehension that obviates confusion and connects him to home and community. (In "Old Boys, Old Girls," the corresponding story in *All Aunt Hagar's Children* that continues his narrative, this is essentially what happens, and Caesar connects to the home and community of his past.)

"A Butterfly on F Street" and "A Dark Night" well fit the overall context of *Lost in the City.* The former depicts black life in Jones's imaginary space of Washington, D.C., and the latter focuses on a character telling black stories. However, it is not possible to force the two stories into the categories above or the one that follows.

The shortest story in the volume, "A Butterfly on F Street," seems to portray a character who is made a better person by some beneficent influence. Mildred Harper meets on the street the woman who stole her recently deceased husband of twenty-seven years and lived with him for the last two years of his life; the woman expresses condolences on Mildred's loss and says "God is with you" before she leaves her in the last paragraph (181). In spite of herself, Mildred can only perfunctorily accept the woman's condolences and well-wishes. Her expression of feeling toward Mildred looks and sounds genuine, implying that a positive influence somewhere in the woman's life has changed her from being a husband stealer and made her better. In the final analysis, it is not at all clear what happened to the woman, but perhaps her change is truly good.

Understanding the story, or at least fully seeing its ambiguity, depends on a close reading of two paragraphs near the end that describe Mildred earlier surreptitiously watching the woman and Mildred's husband outside the woman's house (180). In the first paragraph, the narrator describes Mildred as thinking she sees the woman and her husband walking hand in hand and talking like lovers, but in the second paragraph the narrator says "they were not walking that way at all: The woman was actually holding [the sick] Mansfield's elbow [and helping him into the house]." The story remains ambiguous, but the second paragraph definitely indicates that something, somehow, has happened to change the woman from the husband stealer that she apparently was to the apparently humane person who greets Mildred on the street. ("The Devil Swims Across the Anacostia River," the corresponding story in *All Aunt Hagar's Children,* provides a basis to reinterpret "A Butterfly on F Street" and reach a different conclusion about the woman, but if anything it makes "A Butterfly on F Street" more ambiguous.) It is possible to make some sense of the story's title. In the first paragraph, Mildred is astonished to see a butterfly on F Street that she thought "must have lost its way" (177), and then she expectedly comes face to face with the woman. Maybe the woman has, somehow, found her way morally, and facing her, Mildred is unprepared and out of place like a butterfly in the city that "set[s] off into the traffic heading toward 13th Street."

"A Dark Night" is more straightforward; in it, "back home" stories from the past affect life in Washington in the present. Beatrice Atwell tells her raindrop folk joke/story (225–26) that gets laughs in the present just as it did when her family told it in the past, but it is her macabre, folktale-influenced story of her family members' death by lightning in a dark night "back home" that has the greatest effect. Beatrice seems to internalize the effects of the sinister darkness and death in her story, and at the end her story seems to cut through the superficiality of Mrs. Garrett's earlier implication that she does not believe in "down-home, way-back-when" stories (221). (Mrs. Garrett's story about her conversion in 1894 [225] is self-righteous and not a genuine "back-home" story.) At the end, Beatrice and Mrs. Garrett sit terrified in the darkness in the small, restricted space of Beatrice's bathroom, where they have taken refuge from a storm after Mrs. Garret, afraid to be alone, has pleaded to come into the apartment of the hostile Beatrice, who said at the door, "We ain't no friends no more, or did you forget that?" (227). However, Beatrice's lightning-death story apparently has the power to bring together two women with a strong antagonism for each other in that space, where Mrs. Garrett prays sincerely in the darkness in contrast to her earlier religious pretentiousness. It is not clear whether it is good or bad that stories of the past have an effect in the present, but it is clear that they do have effects. (It is hard to say, however, whether the success or failure of traditional black connection is important as it is in all the stories except "A Butterfly on F Street.")

The three stories that most clearly depict the potential for black connection are "The Store," "A New Man," and "Marie." The latter is the last story in *Lost in the City* and portrays the potential for connection and its necessity the most definitively among all the stories.

The narrative of "The Store," the other first-person story in *Lost in the City,* implies how the idea of black family and community moves from the South to the North, and back and forth, and in the process connects and sustains black people, particularly the narrator. By going back and forth in reference to his dead father's life in Washington and in Columbia, South Carolina, the narrator suggests that he feels supported by his family and community tradition. For example, in an anecdote, the narrator reveals that, when his father was fourteen, one of his first jobs was with an undertaker in Columbia whom the father did not like and who did not like the father. "But, and maybe he got this from [my grandfather], my father figured that he would give the undertaker the best goddamn week of work a fourteen-year-old was capable of. And that's what he did. . . . Then he collected his pay and never went back" (84). Working for the woman at the store in Washington, the narrator plans to pull off the same ironic farce his father did in Columbia, to work one week and "get my pay and tell her to kiss my ass" (87). This is not what the narrator does, but the story of what his father did is part of what connects and sustains the narrator where he is in Washington. (Significantly also, the narrator's voice throughout the story has a characteristic humor that some black people have developed in dealing with the travail of black historical experience.) There is a larger story about the importance of the tradition of black community and black families here, though.

The store where the narrator works at 5th and O streets Northwest becomes a symbol of community and family that is very important for the narrator, the owner Penelope Jenkins, and the other neighborhood black people. The narrator says that, because of "my life at the store, my sense of neighborhood began to expand" (92). At one point, he has dreams of the store in which a line of children extends out the door "until it went out of Washington and into another land" (94). Family pictures of community people make the narrator feel empathy for and a familial closeness to them. He says about one picture: the "more I looked at those smiling girls . . . the more I wanted only good things for them, the way I wanted only good things for my nieces and nephews" (93). Penelope values the pictures, too, and keeps them in her safe "out of harm's way . . . way in back, behind the money" (94). Further, looking in the store window one night, he imagines that he sees his "father coming toward [him]" (103). Particularly, given the reference to the father, one can see that the line of community not only extends "out of Washington and into another land," presumably forward, but it also extends back to the southern tradition of his father, who in a sense is also walking toward the narrator, bringing the tradition to him in Washington. The narrator does not cover up the shortcomings of Penelope and the community people or idealize their actions, and a tragedy in which Penelope accidentally hits and kills a community girl with her car is a turning point that leads to the end of the store's existence. However, the movement of the community forward, the demise of the store notwithstanding, and the back-and-forth pathway of a supportive, sustaining family and community tradition are clear.

The first-person narrator in "All Aunt Hagar's Children," the related, corresponding story in *All Aunt Hagar's Children,* says telling a story is a way of "keeping the world away . . . when the world [gets] too much" (127); the ending of "The Store" shows that this is what the narrator's narrative of family and community does for him. After accidentally killing the community girl, Penelope sadly leaves for good and the narrator will probably never see her again, and the store building becomes the habitation for other businesses and endeavors. At twenty-seven years old, the narrator in the last sentences imagines himself in and around the store among the people the way it used to be. The narrator continues to "keep the world away" through his narrative about community and the families in it. His narrative is imaginative at the end, but so is it before the end. Also, imagination is a large part of why stories "keep the world away" anyhow. The narrator's attraction to community and family and concomitant black cultural tradition is perhaps subconscious, or maybe it is intuitive, but this does not make it less important.

"A New Man" also focuses on the idea of sustaining, connecting journeys and pathways in black tradition, going and coming, coming and going, between the South and the North as fifty-two-year-old Woodrow L. Cunningham immerses himself in a positive process of black connection. There are several symbols of journeys and pathways in the story, including stories, pictures, letters, and memories, and there are actual trips to the North, to the South and back, and forward into the world again. Among the symbols of journeys and pathways, pictures and stories and pictures that are essentially stories are the most positive in the final analysis. Woodrow's development is not complete at the end, but he does achieve something, perhaps a lot.

The first part of the story (203–8) mentions two letters from Woodrow's father in Georgia, describes a fight between Woodrow and his daughter Elaine that will lead to her running away, and depicts Woodrow as a man with heart trouble who would be a "new man" "if he lost thirty or forty pounds" (207). There is some suggestion that the two letters (203, 208) are a pathway and a positive connection between the father in the South and Woodrow in the

North, an implication of movement back and forth that connects and sustains. However, the entirety of the story will show that letters have ambiguous value, which the near-caricature of the father's writing and reading throughout the story and the later burning of Woodrow's own letters in Georgia confirm. As far as the fight with his daughter is concerned, the story suggests that Woodrow is at fault and needs to become a "new man," which he does in the process of looking for his daughter, although he never finds her (at least not physically), and which he does in a process of movement. The process is partly literal, but it is more of a symbolic journey and pathway opened by pictures and stories and by pictures that are stories.

In another section of the story (211–13), Woodrow's wife, Rita, asks "what happened" in the incident with Elaine. Woodrow responds to Rita's question with stories: he "had told the whole story, but then he began to tell her things that had not happened" (212). Woodrow's stories are pathways, ultimately creative, open-ended ones, but still pathways. After this (213–14), Woodrow begins to use different pictures of Elaine as he continues to search for her. One picture, of Elaine in an Easter dress when she was young, gets Woodrow into more and more homes to talk about his daughter. Stories, Woodrow's account as well as the stories the pictures tell, are taking Woodrow on further and further journeys.

The last section of the story (214–16) emphasizes pictures and stories and the stories that pictures can tell. Almost seven years after Elaine disappeared, his father dies and Woodrow goes back to Georgia; the journey to Georgia and back to Washington again shows connection with southern tradition. In his father's trunk in Georgia, Woodrow finds old letters of his written from "the places he worked as he made his way up to Washington" (215). The letters are "all about work" and do not tell much about people, the human story. These letters from the time when Woodrow was moving from the South to the North should reveal a part of a process of sustaining connection, but their limitation because they leave out the human is clear and emphasizes the ambiguous value of letters. His mother's pictures that he finds in his father's trunk have more value: returning to Washington, he brought "back a few of the pictures and none of the letters, which he burned" (216). The stories that his mother's pictures tell are a connection with the picture of his daughter Elaine, the story Elaine's picture tells, and the stories that Woodrow constructs out of Elaine's picture at the end.

The very end shows the picture of Elaine telling stories for Woodrow and opening new pathways for Woodrow and for his stories; Woodrow has become a "new man" through those pathways and stories. "Having lost so much weight, Woodrow felt that even more of the world had opened up to him. And so he wondered if he should go on down 15th Street, try to find a house he had not visited before, and bring out the picture of the child in her Easter dress" (216). This image of Woodrow is not totally positive, but then again he has achieved a lot that is positive, as symbolized by his weight loss. (Perhaps the fact that, in contrast to Woodrow, Rita, who stopped looking for Elaine, got so big that she had to sit in a specially ordered chair [216] puts Woodrow's portrayal in some perspective.) As a "new man," he is different from the one who fought with Elaine, but after she has been gone seven years, it is not clear *which* Elaine he is looking for, the "child in the Easter dress" or the one who ran away, and not clear where he is trying to go in "the world [that] had opened up to him." However, he has already been places in a positive, sustaining, connecting process, and maybe where he is trying to go is an extension of the positive process. "A Rich Man," the corresponding story in *All Aunt Hagar's Children,* brings Elaine back (not back to Woodrow though) and implies through her characterization that the stories about Elaine generated by Woodrow have, somehow, intangibly, extended to her what he got in the positive process. This is one of Jones's most impressive stories. It is thematically intricate, allusive, and nuanced, and its humor stands out.

"Marie" is about memories and stories, and the primary emphasis is on stories generated by memories. "Marie" is the perfect story to end *Lost in the City* because the character Marie connects stories to memories and memories to stories in a process of plot, character, and thematic development that is central in the volume.

Eighty-six-year-old Marie Delaveaux Wilson, the oldest main character in stories that begin with the youngest character, moves from no understanding of the memories and stories of her past, and the black past generally, to a comprehension of their power and importance. The incident that precipitates Marie's development is her slapping of a much younger woman, Vernelle Wise, a receptionist working in the Social Security Office, because Marie has to wait too long for her appointment. Marie's remorse over the incident comes to a head about two weeks later, when she wakes up remembering "a phrase she had not used or heard since her children were small: You whatn't raised that way" (236). This memory seems almost to conjure up the presence of George Carter, a young man from Howard University who wants to record her life story for a class folklore project. She first says "I don't have anything worth talkin about," but he persuades her that "we all got something to say" (237). When George plays back to her the tape of her talking about her father and mother, she tells him she cannot listen to any more when he starts to play the tape's other side. She had never heard a recording of her own voice before, and "nothing had been so stunning in a long, long while, and for a few moments before she found herself, her world turned upside down" (238). She is so fascinated by her voice, "talking about a man [her father] whom she knew as well as her husbands and her sons, a man dead and buried sixty years," that she cries. The power and importance of the story and the memory that connect her to her dead mother and father and other family in her past are obvious.

Marie then has an experience with another story and memory. Holding the hand of the dying boyfriend of her friend Wilamena Mason, she hears his story about Nicodemus, Kansas, "a town where there were only black people" (239), and a woman he was married to for about a year. Some of his story is not clear, but it is clear that the woman and the town "marked him for life": "you should go there and spend some time there." Marie realizes that she was a "complete stranger" (240) to the man and was the last thing he knew in the world, and "now that he was no longer in the world all she knew of him was that Nicodemus place and a lovesick woman [Wilamena] asleep at the foot of his bed. . . . The more she looked at the dead man and the sleeping woman, the more she realized that what she felt was a sense of loss." Although Marie feels a sense of loss, the now-dead man's story and memory connect her with him, Wilamena who loves him, Nicodemus and the historical tradition of all-black towns, the community of Nicodemus that "marked him for life," and the woman he loved there. People, stories, and traditions carry on potentially through people like Marie who live and continue to have memories and tell stories.

Listening again to the tape George Carter had made, Marie tries to connect with Vernelle to learn her story. Marie finds Vernelle's name in the phone book and calls her. She does not say anything when Vernelle's youngest child answers, but by listening to the child, his siblings, and Vernelle talk before Vernelle gets to the phone and she hangs up, Marie hears some of Vernelle's life story unfold over the phone line. Implicitly, present and past, past and present, back and forth, Vernelle's story flows into Marie's and Marie's flows into Vernelle's as Vernelle and her family talk and Marie listens. This all becomes part of Marie's memory and potentially part of the story she can tell.

The end of the story may sound dubious regarding the importance of stories and memories that connect, but it really is not. Marie puts the tapes George has recorded documenting the stages and people in her life in a dresser drawer containing all her valuables: "She knew that however long she lived, she would not ever again listen to them, for in the end, despite all that was on the tapes, she could not stand the sound of her own voice" (243). Her not being able to listen to her own voice is not necessarily bad; instead it probably shows that she feels the momentous power of her own black stories and memories. A process of memory and storytelling that could connect people and communities and carry on tradition has changed Marie and made her a better person in her old age. She had called the Social Security Office several times before she called Vernelle's house, and although she did not answer if Vernelle came on the line at the office, she wanted to apologize to Vernelle by saying, "I whatn't raised that way" (240). In spite of the ending, perhaps the most significant tradition that might be carried on by Marie's memories and stories is the family and communal one that taught her not to do mean things, like slapping Vernelle Wise.

CHAPTER 5

The Stories of *All Aunt Hagar's Children*

There are structural and thematic similarities between Edward P. Jones's first book of short stories, *Lost in the City* (1992), and his second, *All Aunt Hagar's Children* (2006). Each of the fourteen stories in each volume has a direct connection to a corresponding story in the other volume, and a godlike omniscient narrator in twelve of the fourteen stories in the second volume plays a similar role as in twelve stories in the first. (Two stories in both volumes are first-person.) Further, in *All Aunt Hagar's Children,* black people and communities also move from the South to the North. Although there is somewhat less emphasis on symbolic forms such as letters, photographs, and songs than in the first volume, the omniscient narrator still shows the characters' abilities to establish pathways back and forth that are psychological—and sometimes seemingly spiritual, sometimes seemingly psychic or supernatural—that connect people, family, community, and general tradition[1] in the South and North through memories, stories, specific cultural traditions, and history. That is, Washington, D.C., is still the central setting, but consciously, subconsciously,[2] and sometimes literally the characters move back and forth over the journey between the South and the North that they and other black people have taken. The stories are all different, and although not explicit in every story, the establishment of this psychic, supernatural, spiritual back-and-forth road between the South and North that connects people, family, community, and broader tradition is clearly the key to black sustenance and ongoing survival in the second volume as well.

The main difference in *All Aunt Hagar's Children* is an emphasis on the role of creative artists and the theme of artistry. The stories are often more dreamlike, supernatural, experimental, and improvisational because their devices, techniques, or approaches imply and coincide with those of creative artists, who are characters in some stories that have artistry as a theme. Some stories highlight the implication that the omniscient narrator is *a* creative artist, and that Jones himself stands behind the narrator as *the* creative artist. (Getting deeply into the reading of the stories in which artists and artistry become increasingly important, one returns to earlier stories and, because of the overall context, often feels the implied presence of a creative artist and an artist's work where no artist is actually present.) Over the sixteen years since the publication of *Lost in the City,* Jones's short-story writing has evolved to the point where, to a greater extent than in the earlier volume, he highlights, foregrounds, or makes explicit the process of the creative artist and the theme of artistry. Jones has not said that he is a postmodern writer, but it seems that his stories have taken a postmodern turn.[3]

The focus and content of all the stories are by no means the same, though, and there are ways of grouping the stories that show their difference and place the volume's overall difference in the foreground. The most important group consists of stories five, six, seven, and fourteen, which depict creative artists as characters and develop the theme of artistry: "All Aunt Hagar's Children," "A Poor Guatemalan Dreams of a Downtown in Peru," "Root Worker," and "Tapestry." These are the stories that give the volume a thematic direction significantly different from that of *Lost in the City.*

There are additional ways of grouping the stories according to their connection by characters, theme, and structure to stories in *Lost in the City* and their thematic and structural relationship to other stories in *All Aunt Hagar's Children.* Stories four and twelve, "Old Boys, Old Girls," and "A Rich Man," directly link characters and themes to characters and themes in *Lost in the City.* There is a connection between each correspondingly numbered story in the volumes, but in these two stories there is an especially close connection in which a character from *Lost in the City* plays an extended role and the story in *All Aunt Hagar's Children* completes or complements the theme from *Lost in the City*'s story. "Common Law," "Blindsided," and "Bad Neighbors"—stories eight, eleven, and thirteen, respectively—have close connections to corresponding stories in *Lost in the City,* and are similar to the two stories above with close connections in theme and characterization to stories in *Lost in the City.* However, in these three stories, the connections are not especially close. Three others, "In the Blink of God's Eye," "Spanish in the Morning," and "Resurrecting Methuselah"—one, two, and three, respectively—have dreamlike, imaginary, and supernatural characteristics that make them reminiscent of the stories in which the creative artist is present and artistry is a theme. (These three stories and the following two are instances where, after reading into the stories where artistic creation is explicit and after looking at the volume as a whole, the reader, in the general context, feels the implied presence of the creative artist and recognizes the implication of the theme of artistry when they are not explicit.) "Adam Robinson Acquires Grandparents and a Little Sister" and "The Devil Swims Across the Anacostia" are stories nine and ten. The experimentation and improvisation in these two works draw special attention to the role of imagination in their creation, and thus are also reminiscent of stories in which the artist is present and artistry is a theme. The distinction between these stories and the previous three is subtle, and these two are perhaps the hardest to place in any group. The stories do not adhere perfectly to these descriptions, but keeping in mind the broad, general thematic and structural pattern that *All Aunt Hagar's Children* shares with *Lost in the City,* one can use these groups to understand the makeup and dominant thematic direction of the volume.

The ending of "Old Boys, Old Girls" is not definitive, but it is clear that Caesar Matthews is less confused than he was at the end of *Lost in the City*'s "Young Lions" and has the perspective and knowledge to take his life in a much more positive direction. The last paragraph of "Young Lions" begins: "There was something in the air, but he could not make out what it was" (76). In "Old Boys, Old Girls," Caesar finally gets out of Lorton Prison and back in touch with an old girlfriend, Yvonne Miller, whom he loved. When Yvonne dies, Caesar decides to look for "some legit way to pay for [her] funeral" (100). In the final paragraph, he is in the 10th Street neighborhood where he grew up, and trying to decide which way to go. "Down 10th Street was [Abraham] Lincoln's death house [Petersen House, 516 10th Street]. Up 10th was the house where he had been a boy, and where the puppy [his mother had bought would wait] for his father" (101). With a girl watching him, he is flipping a quarter to decide which way to go: "Caesar flipped the quarter. The girl's heart paused. The man's heart paused. The coin reached its apex and then it fell." The conclusion shows that this story is open-ended like "Young Lions," but Caesar does have an affirmative, "legit" purpose that will probably carry him in a positive direction.

When Caesar gets out of prison, the narrator shows him making the connections that will, in a sense, take him back home to the sustenance that he lost in "Young Lions" when he became a thug. He reunites with Yvonne, who is now an "old girl" just as he is now an "old boy," and she helps to reform him with her honest perspective on life: the "sooner people like you stand up and stop the bullshit, then the world can start bein a better place" (93). This perspective, along with her death, which affects him deeply, helps him along the road to becoming "legit." In conjunction with Yvonne's influence and her death, he has a literal and psychological reunion with his family, which also helps create the possibility of his symbolic walk to his old neighborhood and family house at the end.

His brother and his sister reconnect with him to bring him back to them, but Yvonne's death precipitates his own memory of his father's actions when his mother died, reconnecting him with his father as well: "He knelt at the bed and touched Yvonne's shoulder. On a Tuesday morning, a school day, he had come upon his father kneeling at his bed, Caesar's mother growing cold in that bed. His father was crying, and when Caesar went to him his father crushed Caesar to him and took the boy's breath away" (98). Kneeling beside the bed of Yvonne, whom he loves, makes Caesar remember his father kneeling beside the bed of his mother, whom the father loved, and Caesar also remembers his father's actions which showed his love for Caesar. His brother had said, "know that Daddy loves you. It is the one giant truth in the world" (95); Caesar now believes that his father does love him. The reunion with his family by no means goes perfectly, though. Following dinner with his brother and sister's families, he sees the suspicion of his sister, who now lives in the upper-class black Gold Coast, that he could molest her daughter, Caesar's niece, and vomits by his apartment building when he gets out of his sister's car (96). However, after Yvonne's death and the recollection of his father's love, he recovers potentially to move in a positive direction at the end. The possibility of going in the direction of his boyhood community and family house, which symbolize love, is certainly positive, and coincides with the theme of finding connecting, sustaining pathways, which Caesar did not find at the end of "Young Lions."

"Old Boys, Old Girls" develops a character and carries on a theme from a story in *Lost in the City* more fully than any other story in *All Aunt Hagar's Children*. The other story in the volume that has a similar continuity is "A Rich Man," which does not continue the portrayal of the central character in the corresponding story but does give a key role to another character from the earlier story. This character is Elaine Cunningham, the daughter of Woodrow Cunningham in "A New Man" in *Lost in the City*. She is not physically present after the story's beginning but figures thematically throughout the story.

Horace Perkins, who always thinks he is "rich" because he is old and still has many sexual relationships, only becomes truly rich after Elaine gives him a real "story." Near the end of "A Rich Man," as his apartment lay in shambles, a symbol of the truth of his life, Elaine asks Horace, "What happened?" (344). Her mother, Rita, asks her father, Woodrow, the same question—"What happened? Whatcha say to her?" (211–12)—in "A New Man" regarding the reason why Elaine ran away. Woodrow "told the whole story, but then he began to tell her things that had not happened" (212). Woodrow is not lying when he creates new stories about what happened. These new stories are inseparable from the story of his past, which is grounded in the black tradition of the South in

Georgia; the new stories carry on the past and are part of what opens up pathways to the future and makes him "a new man."

On the other hand, in spite of what he had thought about his "rich" life, Horace has no substantive story grounded in black tradition as Woodrow does. Sitting in his apartment amid its debris, he searches for a story, essentially finding himself in the dark when he does: "My name is Horace Perkins, he thought just as the sun set. My name is Horace Perkins, and I worked many a year at the Pentagon. The apartment became dark, but he did not have it in him to turn on the lights" (343). Later, when Elaine asks him "what happened," he shows that he has no answer or real "story" to tell. He only responds by physically assaulting and threatening to kill her because he holds her responsible for trashing his apartment. She calms Horace down by begging him not to kill her in front of her infant baby, who she says is "innocent of everything" (344), and by assuring him that she could never be responsible for what happened to the apartment. The narrator says, "How does a man start over with nothing? Horace thought. Elaine came near him, and the baby still watched him as his crying lessened. How does a man start from scratch?" (345). Elaine says further, "I would not hurt you for anything in the world, Horace. . . . You been too good to me for me to hurt you like this, Horace." Ironically, he does not have to start from scratch now because there is a "story" of love and caring in what Elaine says to Horace and what she does, and this is the "story" that can truly make him "a rich man."

Reading and comparing "A New Man" and "A Rich Man," one sees that there must be a cryptic relationship in which the essence of the "newness" that Woodrow achieves through his stories by the end of "A New Man" gets somehow transferred to his daughter Elaine, although he has not seen her for seven years, so that she can tell a loving, caring "story" that makes Horace a "rich man." A primary story Woodrow is telling about Elaine by the end features the beneficent symbol of "the child in the Easter dress" (216). It is possible to read both stories in different ways, but clearly Elaine becomes the positive connection between Woodrow's "newness" and Horace's "richness." Through Horace Perkins in "A Rich Man," Elaine complements the theme of "A New Man," and brings it together thematically with "A Rich Man."

Three other stories in *All Aunt Hagar's Children,* "Common Law," "Blindsided," and "Bad Neighbors," clearly complement the thematic development of the corresponding stories in *Lost in the City.* "Common Law" and "Bad Neighbors" portray characters from the first volume who play some role, but not a major one. In "Blindsided," no significant character from *Lost in the City* plays a direct role; the connection is primarily thematic.

Comparing "Common Law" and its corresponding story, *Lost in the City*'s title story, one sees that Georgia Evans (a minor character in "Lost in the

City") finds her sustaining, connecting pathways that Lydia Walsh in "Lost in the City" is just too "lost" to find. (Lydia is a little girl with a minor role in "Common Law.") At the end, Lydia, a lawyer, goes riding through the streets of her childhood; this is a symbolic act of going into her past to imagine it as a part of a story that can then move her forward. However, she seems largely at a dead end, not having imagined a sustaining story. In contrast to Lydia, Georgia in "Common Law," Lydia's mother's friend, is a maid in Washington who had "never seen any sky but the sky over Scottsboro, Alabama" (203), before she left home. Further, "Common Law" details the abuse that Georgia suffers and tolerates from her live-in boyfriend, Kenyon Morrison. However, the people in the black community literally walk Kenyon out of the neighborhood by crowding around him and forcing him down the streets and away from Georgia (234–35). Then the "people on Ridge Street became afraid that Kenyon would come back and hurt Georgia, so they started looking out for her, driving her to and from work" (236). Randy Comstock, the man driving Georgia to work at the end, calls himself a "real man [who] can defer to his wife and still be a real man" (237). Shortly before, in an act of prolepsis, the narrator had looked ahead "one and a half years" (236) and then "more than eight years" to the time of Georgia's two marriages; the narrator concludes the story with another look into the future of Georgia's life centered by more words from Randy: "She was just about thirty years from seeing her first grandchild come into the world. 'A little give and a little take make a good marriage, my mama always said.' She was more than forty and a half years from death" (237). (Georgia in "Lost in the City" "would never have children of her own" (149), but she is the same character in "Common Law" who will have a grandchild.)

Georgia has a past that goes back to Scottsboro, Alabama, but it is the community in the present that saves her from abuse and, in the context of Randy's words, prepares her to have a family in the future. As the narrator implies at the end, she does have a life story grounded in the community and concomitantly in family that will sustain her and carry her along. Lydia is a Yale graduate and world traveler who made "more [money] than all her ancestors put together" (*Lost* 148; *Aunt Hagar's* 236–37), but Georgia has more than Lydia ever has.

"Blindsided" portrays Roxanne Stapleton, who evolves from figurative blindness when she has sight to moral sight, when confronted with truth, after she becomes mysteriously blind; in Gospel" from *Lost in the City,* Vivian L. Slater has sight but, confronted by truth, becomes figuratively blind instead of seeing the truth. The truth that both women face is that they are not better than other people, particularly her so-called friend Diane McCollough in Vivian's case, and her supporter Agnes Simmons in Roxanne's case.

Roxanne generally thinks and acts like Vivian in "Gospel" for much of "Blindsided," but the important change happens at the end of the latter story. Roxanne is from "nine ugly miles outside Baton Rouge"; promising to be back for breakfast, she left her family and her three-year-old daughter "in the middle of the night with two men friends" (301) and flippantly, haphazardly, made her way to Washington, having returned only once since then. She is an attractive woman and looks down on and abuses Agnes, who "no one had [called] beautiful" (303) since her long-ago boyfriend who was looking for sex. Roxanne changes when a man sexually assaults her, and she calls out to Agnes after hearing "a little voice [call] her name" (318): "Please, Agnes, is that you? Agnes?" The person she hears is a little girl named Adele Benoit whose "tiny voice" (319) makes the man stop. Adele later says, "You want me to stay with you, Miss Roxanne? We all be missin Miss Agnes," who has left town (319). The realization of the need for Agnes gives the still-blind Roxanne moral sight. She thinks of "that once upon a time [when she] could stand in front of that classroom nine ugly miles from the capital of Louisiana" (321) and recite the name of the planets. At the end, Roxanne reveals her moral sight in a figuration using Pluto: On the planet, "she would put a sign that said Pluto was open all the time to all of God's children. Yes, open even to the least of them."

"Blindsided" thematically complements "Gospel" by showing a positive evolution to moral sight as opposed to continued blindness to truth. Roxanne has a past in Louisiana, has journeyed to Washington, has traveled back to Louisiana once, and after she is blind gets Adele's brother to write to her parents and daughter inviting them to Washington for Christmas (315). In spite of the frivolity she showed in leaving Louisiana and coming to Washington, the connection to the past and literal and figurative back-and-forth movement between Louisiana and Washington are significant because they are part of black tradition. In the context of Jones's stories, and in light of the narrator's reference to the classroom in Louisiana near the end, this tradition gives her sustenance that goes along with the moral sight that she attains. Variations on themes of morality are apparent throughout Jones's work, but these themes are especially clear as *All Aunt Hagar's Children* develops with the presentation of stories such as "Blindsided." Somewhat ironically, this story about a woman who goes suddenly, mysteriously blind is one in which the humor is very entertaining.

Among the stories "Common Law," "Blindsided," and "Bad Neighbors," the latter has the most tangential connection to the corresponding story in *Lost in the City*. Sharon Palmer's ability to "see" in the dark at the end of "Bad Neighbors" loosely picks up on the image of Beatrice Atwell, also a minor character in "Bad Neighbors," sitting in the dark at the end of "A Dark Night" in *Lost in the City.*

"Bad Neighbors" makes it clear that Sharon learns what it means to be a "bad neighbor," in a sense learns to "see" in the dark. Many years after her family and others successfully conspire to get the lower-class Bennington family out of their middle-class neighborhood, Derek Bennington unexpectedly comes out of the night to save Sharon from physical and sexual assault. After this happens, she stands in the dark in her condominium but truly "sees" the reality of black class prejudice: the "idea that [Derek Bennington] had been there [following her to protect her] . . . out there in the dark offering no sign and no sound, out there for months and perhaps years of her life, seemed to give her something to measure her life by. But she did not know how to do that. After she turned out the bathroom light, she stood in the dark for a long time" (373). Sharon is standing in the dark and still does not know how to "measure her life," but although her conscious understanding of her life may not be complete, she now "sees" and understands. In the dark room as she gets into bed with her husband, a medical student at Howard University, Sharon implies that she "sees" the world differently, to the extent that she can be a "good neighbor." Further, the narrator may indicate that Derek Bennington, as a lower-class black person, symbolizes what is "out there in the dark" following upwardly mobile black people like Sharon, not to bring them down as they fear, but as a supportive foundation.

The first three stories in *All Aunt Hagar's Children,* "In the Blink of God's Eye," "Spanish in the Morning," and "Resurrecting Methuselah," imply the presence and creative work of artists in the context of reading all the volume's stories. That is, after encountering creative artists, the theme of creative artistry, and the implication of formal artistic practice in later stories, one looks back at these early stories and notices in them a similar artistic practice. The imaginary, dreamlike, and supernatural in the later stories, which are implicitly the devices of creative artists who are characters in the stories, appear in the early stories, too.

In the language and figurations of "In the Blink of God's Eye," there are several examples of an imaginary, dreamlike, and somewhat supernatural quality that one, looking back in retrospect, would see as the conscious practice of the creative writer, here implicitly the godlike omniscient narrator. The following about Ruth Patterson and her husband Aubrey from the beginning of the story is an example: "That 1901 winter when the wife and her husband were still new to Washington, there came to the wife like a scent carried on the wind some word that wolves roamed the streets and roads of the city after sundown. . . . Still, the night, even in godforsaken Washington, sometimes had that old song that could pull Ruth up and out of her bed, the way it did when she was a girl across the Potomac River in Virginia where all was safe and all was family" (1).

The ending of the story depicting Aubrey is a better example: "He halted at the mouth of the bridge, the land of Washington, D.C., spread out forever and ever before him. . . . Ruth's husband could hear voices now, and he shuddered. He turned in the saddle to see the southern road so many would travel on to reach that land just across the river. He saw nothing but the horse tracks in the snow, growing fainter with each second as more and more snow covered them. The voices hushed. His boots touched the horse's sides ever so gently. The horse stepped onto the bridge to Washington. . . . Ruth's husband patted [the horse's] neck. The top button on his coat came loose again and he rebuttoned it, thankful that his hand had not yet stiffened up. His heart was pained, and it was pain enough to overwhelm a city of men" (30). Jones's stories often have somewhat similar qualities of the imaginary, dreamlike, and supernatural. However, these qualities are more greatly highlighted here, and in the context of later stories featuring creative artists and artistry, the same conscious, formal, artistic practices stand out.

This is the quintessential Jones story because it focuses on the black tradition and the journeys and pathways between the South and the North, between the North and the South, which historically sustain black people. Aubrey looks back on "the southern road so many would travel on to reach that land just across the river," the road south that he has traveled and from which he is now returning. He feels pain because this is an arduous, perilous journey, but it is also the connecting lifeline of black people. Aubrey and Ruth have a troubled relationship in the story, but as Aubrey looks back on the southern road, the larger reality of black people transcending oppression through their connection of the present with the past and immersion in black tradition is more important than a personal relationship. The story captures a sense of a connecting, sustaining past, and at the same time suggests the black tradition to which black people need to establish pathways: "[Aubrey] came from a land where human beings had a past as tangible as dirt, where even children with no parents or grandparents had laps they could cry into" (11). Miles Patterson from "The Girl Who Raised Pigeons," the corresponding story in *Lost in the City,* is also a character in this story. He is the orphan, found by Ruth in a bundle hanging in a tree, his umbilical cord still attached, and named after Aubrey's dead father, to whom the narrator's words about parentless children would apply. "In the Blink of God's Eye" is a snapshot of black survival against oppression.

In spite of being a very young girl starting kindergarten, the first-person narrator in "Spanish in the Morning" at times sounds like the writer conscious of using her imagination to create; one specific instance of creation is the image of her family on the road between the South and the North. The narrator says that when

> I was two and a half years old, my father sat me on his lap and we spent part of an afternoon going through his *Life* magazines. In one there was an article on proletarian art in the Soviet Union. In my imagination my grandmother and my father and my aunts were to become like the statue in a picture in that article. There was a road that southern people took to get to Washington, and on that road there were four of them. My grandmother had one hand pointing ahead. She wore a bonnet and a long pioneer-woman dress. My two aunts, each carrying a bundle, were looking to where she was pointing, and their hands were shading their eyes like that lady in Mexico [that she imagined earlier] waiting for her children. One of my father's hands was in my grandmother's hand, lest he run away, and his other hand was pointing back, a boy frozen in photograph-gray. (41–42)

The girl is imagining her life in specific detail when she was two and a half, but she also imagines her life at "four weeks old" (32) and "eight months old." This ubiquitous-like knowledge goes along with the implication that she could be creating this story, "Spanish in the Morning," about her family. In the context of the later stories about artists and artistry, there are many instances in "Spanish in the Morning" that imply that the girl could create and is creating this very story using her imagination.

The image in her imagination of the girl's family on the southern road is like the one at the end of "In the Blink of God's Eye," and there is a similar point in the two stories about the literal and figurative road from the South to the North, back and forth, and the consequent sustaining connection. The girl's mother "came from a line of Washingtonians who saw education as a right God had given their tribe the day after he gave Moses the Ten Commandments" (33), but she says her story is more about her father's side of the family, which is from "that place five miles outside of Columbia, South Carolina." That South Carolina place, which her paternal grandfather migrates to Washington from during the story, is the important connection. In spite of the middle-class, lower-class division between her mother and father's sides of the family, this connection to the traditional past allows the girl to imagine a chain of family members who support and sustain her: "[My mother] was joined in my mind by my father and then by both my grandfathers and my mother's people and all my father's people, all of them coming to get me" (39). ("Spanish in the Morning" does not have a human character in common with "The First Day," the corresponding story in *Lost in the City*. The common "character" is a school, Walker-Jones Elementary, where the little girl in "The First Day" is forced to go and where the father in "Spanish in the Morning" wants his daughter to go.)

"Resurrecting Methuselah" is the most atypical among Jones's stories because it adheres the least to his dominant thematic patterns. The one clear thematic similarity to the body of Jones's stories is its depiction of journeys back and forth through time and to various geographical locations. The story does not set these journeys in the context of black history and tradition, but it does depict journeys more generally.

"Resurrecting Methuselah" is similar to "In the Blink of God's Eye" and "Spanish in the Morning" because of its structure and thematic presentation that are experimental and imaginary or dreamlike. Throughout its entirety, the reality of the story takes various forms—for example, actual dreams, supposedly "real life" descriptions, memories, and a poster picture depicting "The Life of Methuselah"—but from the very beginning of the story to the very end, its reality is seldom clearly distinguishable from imagination or dream. Most of the first paragraph describes a widely encompassing scene from Okinawa, Japan, to Washington to "142 years before that night [when] a man who had been a slave" (53) built a chair in which a character sits. The scene is partly realistic because it describes Sergeant Percival Channing having sex with a prostitute in Okinawa and his wife, Anita Hughes Channing, in Washington taking care of their sick daughter, Bethany, but it is also imaginative and dreamlike because it puts together such a montage of disparate people and places, especially in its reference to the ex-slave who built the chair. After Anita "allow[s] her mind to drift somewhat" thinking about the time difference between Washington and Okinawa, and sees Bethany "go away into sleep," in the next paragraph the realities of sex with a prostitute in Okinawa and Anita caring for Bethany in Washington merge into the dream of Bethany and the dream reality of Methuselah. "What the sergeant her husband did with the prostitute, he had not done with the mother of his child in nearly six months, and he would not do it ever again. Neither the sergeant nor his wife knew this as their only child turned in exhaustion onto her right side and entered a dream where Methuselah was waiting, not centuries old, not even a man, but waiting as a little girl who merely wanted to play" (54).

Schoolteacher Methuselah Harrington, named after the biblical Methuselah, is an integral part of the imaginary dream life of the story. The children "found it hard not to relate the man named Methuselah on the poster with the teacher Mr. Methuselah who led them in the Lord's Prayer every morning and who told them how the people in Lapland lived day to day amid snow and reindeer and darkness a good part of the year" (57). Methuselah Harrington also tells the children that the only reason people cannot live longer than Methuselah, "live till five thousand years" (65), is that they lack faith. Methuselah on the poster is "spry-looking" (57) at ninety. At ninety-one he is "faltering" (58), but also at ninety-one with Jesus behind him, "Methuselah was spry again," as he was at one hundred, two hundred, nine hundred, and nine hundred and one years old. Methuselah Harrington's words, actions, and conflation with the biblical Methuselah on the poster, along with his name association with Methuselah in Bethany's dream, make him surreal, imaginary, and dreamlike in the story's general context.

Throughout the story, Anita has memories from her earlier life, such as getting pregnant "three months before she was to enter nursing school" (53), and remembers trips that she seems actually to take; however, near the end, Anita suggests that she might be imagining her life or that it might be a dream. She takes a trip to Okinawa to see Sergeant Channing that she mysteriously, inexplicably cuts short in Honolulu and returns to Washington (67–71). On the way home, Anita "began to feel that she had slept through something and now that she was awake, she had to make do with what she now had" (71). Particularly at this point near the end after the story has developed a highly imaginary, dreamlike quality, one wonders if the trip is imaginary or even a dream, and if Anita is coming out of a state of imagination or waking up from a dream.

Apparently awake in the last section of the story (71–73), Anita takes a trip to Walter Reed Hospital with Bethany to visit the sick Sergeant Channing, but the ending of the story makes it unclear whether she is really awake and whether she and the story itself ever emerge from the region of imagination and dream. Leaving Walter Reed, she saw "a curious side street in Bethesda, that she had seen one busy, crowded day as she took Wisconsin Avenue into Maryland, and she had told herself that one day she and Bethany would explore that most inviting street and not even care that much if they got lost. What time could be better than today? What time could be better than what might be the last day of five thousand years?" (73). The story ends on this "curious side street," with a cryptic reference to what Methuselah Harrington says about people being able to live five thousand years. This side street seems to be in an imaginary or dream world more than a real one, and the allusion to Methuselah Harrington's words seems to confirm that Anita is in an imaginary or dream world of the five-thousand-year life of Methuselah. (Anita Hughes Channing could be the same Anita Hughes from "The Night Rhonda Ferguson Was Killed" in *Lost in the City,* but they have very few similar personal characteristics.)

This conflation of reality into a form not distinguishable from imagination or dream suggests, in the context of later stories in the volume, the presence and creation of the artist, implicitly the godlike omniscient narrator, who experiments with the construction of an imaginary or dream world. This very atypical Jones story is cryptic and difficult, but it is among his most interesting.

"The Devil Swims Across the Anacostia River" and "Adam Robinson Acquires Grandparents and a Little Sister" have similarities to the three stories last discussed, and the distinction between them is somewhat arbitrary, although not totally. In "The Devil Swims," experimentation and improvisation draw attention to the implied imaginative creation of an artist; although "Adam Robinson" may not be as experimental and improvisational, the same thing is true about this story. Again, the implied creation resides in the context of other stories in *All Aunt Hagar's Children* in which artists are characters and artistry is a theme, and in which experimentation and improvisation imply similar imaginative creation.

It is somewhat obvious that imagination is at the forefront of "The Devil Swims" and that it is experimental and improvisational when the Devil, declaring his name "Himself," having swum across the Anacostia River, appears in Washington to confront a woman, Laverne Shepherd (271); the challenge is using imagination to experiment and improvise while shaping a story from such an unusual situation involving such an improbable character. The omniscient narrator, the implied writer, successfully imagines the story. From the beginning, the reader does not know where this story is going or how it can get there, but at the end feels that the story has developed well. As usual in Jones's stories, there is ambiguity at the end, but the story still comes together thematically and structurally.

"The Devil Swims" is similar to other stories in the two volumes because it focuses on family connection, this time somewhat paradoxically, however, a common connection the women in Laverne's family have with the Devil, and because it conjoins briefly but significantly with the corresponding story in *Lost in the City,* "A Butterfly on F Street." As part of the narrator's experimental and improvisational imagination of the story, Laverne imagines several facts and events of her female family connection with the Devil and imagines her connection, too. "Both her grandmothers had come to know the Devil so well that he, in all his guises, called them always by their childhood nicknames" (272). The "Devil had a special thing for the women on both sides of her family, a thing born with Eve" (275). Fourteen years earlier on a Maryland beach on the Atlantic Ocean, a voice had challenged her paternal grandmother: "Did you come all this way to lose your faith, to drop down into the bottom of the sea? Ahead of you is this water and behind you he's [the Devil's] coming? Did you lose your faith?" (276). Her grandmother walks into the ocean and walks on water, like Jesus, until she disappeared "on the horizon" (278–79). The Devil "was forever on [the grandmothers'] minds, but Laverne had tried to live in a different world. . . . She wished she had picked up a trick or two for dispelling him, for getting on with the rest of her life" (281). After the Devil disappears after promising to return to Laverne, the last paragraph in the story leaves her moral fate ambiguous, as she "waded into the crowd [on the street], and the current of the colored people was so strong that it simply carried her on up the road" (292).

However, evidence from earlier in "The Devil Swims" and a close comparative reading of sections from *Lost in the City*'s "A Butterfly on F Street" suggest that Laverne has done something good that will make her moral fate positive. "On Maple View, she had befriended a dying man, Mansfield Harper, had even held his hand in those moments before he died the evening Mansfield's woman [the lover he left his wife for] had stepped away on an errand. . . . But all that good had not paid off this day [when the Devil accosted her]" (*All Aunt Hagar's Children* 274–75). Maybe it has not "paid off," but in the context of the brief quotation above and the actions of Mansfield's lover, who seems to show genuine moral concern for Mansfield's deserted wife throughout "A Butterfly on F Street," Laverne's actions might have "paid off" morally. Somehow, although it is never clear exactly how in either story, Mansfield's lover is transformed to goodness after Laverne's moral act and again, although it is by no means clear, one could argue that Laverne's kindness to a dying man means that she could be saved from the Devil, in spite of what she thinks. (The relationship between the stories in the two volumes is close at the specific point where Laverne remembers her interaction with Mansfield Harper, although "The Devil Swims" does not clear up the ambiguity of either story.)

"Adam Robinson" is experimental because it purports to be a different kind of story that is not imaginary, dreamlike, and supernatural; further, the narrator virtually "announces" the experimentation with the very first word of the story, "Tuesday," alone at the top of the page. A designated day of the week, alone by itself, before thirteen major sections throughout the story provide a structural form that appears nowhere else in Jones's short stories, creating a sense that the narrator is speaking in a more straightforward, realistic, and objective voice than in other stories. Whether or not it is as realistic, straightforward, and objective as it purports to be, "Adam Robinson" achieves the distinction of standing out singly among Jones's stories because of how its structured narrative looks on the page and because, within this structure, the narrative sounds more straightforward, realistic, and objective; so the experiment succeeds. (The story's full title, "Adam Robinson Acquires Grandparents and a Little Sister," a complete descriptive sentence, suggests the experimentation to achieve straightforwardness, realism, and objectivity.)

As all the stories in *All Aunt Hagar's Children* do, "Adam Robinson" complements a corresponding story in *Lost in the City,* in this case, "His Mother's House"; the narrator in "Adam Robinson" is responding to the theme of fractured family, community, and tradition in the story from *Lost in the City.* Adam Robinson is a minor character in "His Mother's House" who for a brief time lives with Joyce Moses, because his mother leaves him at Joyce's house to pay off her dope-dealer son Santiago for a drug debt (*Lost* 160). In "Adam Robinson," one learns that, ironically, living at Joyce's house gave Adam at least an uneasy feeling of "home" that he did not have living with his own dope-addicted father and mother. Joyce's own family members do not have a sense of "home" at Joyce's, though, and so drugs have fractured her family and Adam's too. The narrator in "Adam Robinson" tries to heal the fracture by bringing Adam "home" to his own biological family, represented by his paternal grandfather Noah Robinson, Noah's wife Maggie, and Adam's sister Elsa, and detaching him from the tenuous memory of "home" that Joyce's house is for him. The last daily heading in the story is "Sunday," and Noah is in church with Adam, Maggie, and Elsa. In the last paragraph, "Adam held on to Noah's coat, for he knew it was possible for people to rise up and disappear out of his life" (270). It seems that Noah has psychologically reconnected his grandson Adam with his biological family and symbolically brought him back "home." The narrator does, in a sense, heal the fracture in family and community in "His Mother's House," as well as the fractured feeling about family that Adam still has, when Adam "acquires" grandparents and a sister in "Adam Robinson."

There is an underlying theme in the story of sustaining connection and continuity relating to black family, community, and tradition. One example, going back to the South, is the family line and life of Noah, now in his sixties, who had come to Washington from South Carolina when he was seven, still "pining for South Carolina" (239–40). Maggie's family line does not go back to the South, but the longevity of her marriage to Noah is another example. Maggie was "a woman with more than two hundred years of Washingtonians behind her" (241); they "had been married forty-five years" (242). An example of connection and continuity not directly related to family, community, or tradition is the description of Noah's bonsai tree: "A booklet that came with the tree said it had been 'trained' for thirty-five years. He had waited the first two years for the tree to wither and die, but it went on and on. Now he believed that it could live forever. In the National Arboretum he and Maggie had seen bonsai trees that had been living—'trained'—for three hundred, four hundred, five hundred years" (260).

"All Aunt Hagar's Children," "A Poor Guatemalan Dreams of Downtown Peru," "Root Worker," and "Tapestry" are the four stories that make the role of artists and the theme of artistry clear; these stories create the context for seeing these themes in other stories in the volume where they are implied and not explicit. "All Aunt Hagar's Children," the title story and the fifth one in the volume, is where the emphasis on artists and artistry becomes very apparent.

The story the first-person narrator tells by the end of "All Aunt Hagar's Children" is a mystery story in which he largely solves the mystery; it is a story that encompasses the black experience but that is also universal because it is much more than black. The story develops from detective work the narrator does on a specific case, from things that he knows about his family history, from what he learns about his own personal life and relationships, and from a haunting incident on the street involving a white woman.

The threads of the mystery are all intertwined, part of the larger, universal mystery story that is "All Aunt Hagar's Children." The narrator works for a lawyer who sometimes does detective work and was in the military police in Korea, but he is not a detective. However, early in the story, with the urging of his mother, he agrees to help his mother's friend, Miss Agatha, find the killer of her son Ike Appleton (105–8). Also early in the story, he starts his version of the account of what happened in his relationship with Sheila Larkin, whom he had told "as kindly as I could that she and I were finished" (103); starts the story of the white woman he saw dying while mysteriously saying, *"A moll is gav vain ah rav und ah rabbit sin"* (105); and introduces the story of his Aunt Penny and his mother beating the white man who tried to rape Miss Agatha in Alabama when they were girls, forcing them to have to flee to Washington (108–9).

The narrator senses his full storytelling power and begins to use it as the story develops; the key moment when he feels and starts to use his power is when his employer's wife, Dvera Jaffe, reveals the identity of the mysterious white woman, Miriam Sobel, whom he saw die in the street (127). "Now that I had a name to go with my memory, her dying words were louder than ever. In my head, the woman Miriam Sobel rose up and stood in the streetcar tracks, just as she had before she began to fall, and set her wig in place" (127). With Miriam rising and standing "in [his] head," he essentially becomes the storyteller who can bring his stories and the people in them to life, although he is not yet fully conscious of what he can do.

After this, he gives a final account of his relationship with Sheila Larkin that implies that his thoughts about her are defensive and self-serving because he misused her, and finishes telling the story of who killed Ike; the story of his mother, Aunt Penny, and Miss Agatha in Alabama; and most significantly the story of Miriam Sobel. After drinking four beers and leaving a bar, the narrator sees Sheila and one of her sisters on the street walking arm in arm and prepares for a confrontation. However, they walk by and do not notice him, and "it wasn't as if they had unlocked arms and walked around me, or stayed arm in arm and walked together around me to the left or the right. It was simply as if they had walked through me, still talking, still arm in arm" (128–29). The narrator could be drunk and hallucinating, but he has made such a big deal of avoiding Sheila before this and now of preparing to confront her because deep within himself he knows that he is wrong for mistreating her. Sheila having gone on with her life, as indicated by her walking through him as if he were not there, highlights the narrator's inner guilt shown by his still being so fixated on her. The narrator does not understand the meaning of what happened on the street with Sheila and her sisters, but his account of the incident reveals the truth. Very shortly afterwards, his storytelling power seems to grow and become more conscious as he first does some real detective work and discovers and reveals who killed Ike, his own wife, Alona, (129–30), probably because he was unfaithful (118–22). Then he finishes recounting what happened to his aunt, mother, and Miss Agatha in Alabama, not necessarily with the facts, but more certainly with a *story* like the one a storyteller would create to bring everything to a good conclusion. He says that the white man his mother and aunt beat for trying to rape Miss Agatha regained consciousness, said God was responsible for what happened to him, converted to religion, and became a preacher: "The law let it be, and the world the white people had made for themselves was set right again" (131).

Making sense of the Miriam Sobel story is the most important thing. All the words he heard Miriam say were: "*A moll is gav vain ah rav und ah rab-bit sin. . . . Zetcha kender lock gadank za tire vos ear lair rent doe*" (126). Dvera Jaffe gives him a translation of the Yiddish words: "*Once upon a time there was a rabbi and his wife. . . . Listen, children, remember, precious ones, what you're learning here*" (131). Dvera says: "They were my father's words, his way of beginning stories to me. All his stories started that way. He used to tell me stories when the world got too much. Comforting, you know. Keeping the world away" (127). Telling stories to "keep the world away" is one thing that the storyteller does, and the significance of telling stories is what the narrator learns from Miriam's words and his encounter with her, which makes sense of her part of the mystery story and further opens her story up to him as a storyteller at the end.

The narrator does not say explicitly that he realizes his role as a storyteller who "keeps the world away" but does suggest that he understands the miraculous power of storytelling. In the last paragraph, Dvera gives the narrator a photograph of a younger Miriam with her family, which he takes to the window "where the light was better" (132), thus already indicating somewhat of a figurative transformation of her story. However, a greater indication of his transformative power as a storyteller occurs as he looks from the picture of Miriam's family to the street where he sees "six little colored girls," thus conflating the image of Miriam's family with the image of the girls. He describes one girl: "Her long plaits swung with her in an almost miraculous way. It was good to watch her, because I had never seen anything like that in Washington in my whole life. I followed her until she disappeared. It would have been nice to know what was on her mind."

He says it "would have been nice to know what was on [the girl's] mind," but instead of closing off the possibility of knowing, he leaves open the possibility of creating further stories about the girl, Miriam Sobel, and others with the "miraculous power" he has as a storyteller. He indicates his realization of this power when he says that he has "never seen anything like that in Washington in my whole life." The new vision is the creative artist's transformative vision. He will not have to make a trip to Alaska "to hunt for gold" now (105) because "there was nothing else for me to discover" in Washington. There is plenty to discover in Washington with his now-realized creative power. In fact, he has already creatively "discovered" a lot. He has told the story of the Jewish woman Miriam Sobel, an oppressed woman and a member of a traditionally oppressed group, who ultimately triumphs by rising, standing, and coming to life "in [the narrator's] head" (127) and then again figuratively coming to life in the conflated image with the girls at the end (132), and he has made Miriam's story the center for the other stories about oppressed black people, stories which are largely triumphant, too. He thus miraculously transforms black stories of oppression in Alabama and Washington into an encompassing universal story of triumph over oppression. Including the black characters in this story and Miriam among "all Aunt Hagar's children," the narrator could go further to tell other universal stories of triumph over oppression.[4]

The narrator's universal story that goes beyond the black experience is a positive story of triumph that "comforts" and "keeps the world away," as Dvera says stories should do. The narrator embodies this story because he becomes a better human being, especially with regard to his attitude toward women (as implied in the Sheila Larkin incident), at the same time that he becomes aware of his ability to create stories that can "keep the world away." (The narrator's Aunt Penny in this story is the same Penelope Jenkins from "The Store" in *Lost in the City* who "owned a grocery store at 5th and O Streets, N.W." [*Aunt Hagar's Children* 104], but she has almost no similarity to the character in "The Store." There is not much similarity between the two stories, either.)

In "A Poor Guatemalan Dreams of a Downtown in Peru," it is difficult to distinguish the realistic, actual events of Arlene Baxter's life from the dreamlike, imaginary, supernatural world of her artistic creation in which she miraculously escapes death many times, but in the final analysis it is the dreamlike, imaginary, supernatural *story* that Arlene creates, her story of miracles that perpetuates her life and all life, that is important. For most of "A Poor Guatemalan," Arlene creates a predominantly fictional world in which she cannot believe her defiance of death in her own fiction, and her fiction also defies the reader's realistic belief. During the story, she reveals the process of artistic creation that is more important than the realistic and actual, and by the end she understands the significance of her story. Because it is so dreamlike, imaginary, and supernatural, "A Poor Guatemalan" is *the* most experimental and difficult to understand story in *All Aunt Hagar's Children;* beyond the depiction of the theme of artistry, the story implies the role of creators very aggressively experimenting. The implied creators are Arlene, the omniscient narrator, and Jones too because of some specifics in the story.

For the first seven pages of the story (133–40), it is not at all clear that Arlene is creating a fictional story; the first clear indication that she is creating two stories is when the narrator, sometimes in parentheses to represent the separation of the fictional from the actual, begins to talk about the daily events that Arlene is recording in her diary that are, to some extent at least, distinguishable from the fictional. Some of the diary descriptions are: "Arlene at eighteen wrote whimsically in her diary while at Holy Cross [College]" (140); "she wrote in her diary at thirty in Washington, D.C." (140–41); "she wrote in the diary her second week at Holy Cross" (141); "at twenty-two, she would write in her diary [about what was going on in her other fictional life]" (145); "in the diary entry, she would also feel safe in not counting [an escape of death in her fictional life]"; "and in the diary Arlene did not count [another escape of death in her fictional life]"; and "Arlene described in her diary [her relationship with a character she created in her fictional life]" (155). It is not easy to separate Arlene's actual life from the fictional that she creates because the difference is subtle, and the actual and fictional converge many times. Close reading shows there is a difference between the fictional and the actual, though.

After the second paragraph, when the narrator describes Arlene talking about her first miraculous escape of death at eight years old, some of the description is about actual, real events in her life which she records in the diary, at the same time that the description highlights the miraculous events that are her fictional life story as an artist. The description of her first escape of death by drowning conflates her life of the miraculous with the miraculous in a biblical story, indicating the fictional that is separate from the daily life of her diary: "The Israelites who found safe passage through the parted Red Sea could testify as to what it was like next. A shallow path of easy water presented itself and Arlene was pushed quite peacefully to the other side, her stomach heavy with a quart or more of creek water. She was exhausted once she hit the shore and did not move once there, her body expelling the water a spoonful at a time. She was eight years and two weeks, and this was the first miracle" (135). Placing Arlene in the context of the long-ago Israelites walking through the sea parted with walls of water on both sides makes it clearer that the part of her story about miracles is fictional. Although the narrator says "just about everything before that day [of the first escape from death] at the creek was like something from a dream, a dream of some eight years" (134), the true dream of her life starts with the creation of fiction when she is eight years old.

Two other characters who seem to be separate, discrete people also could be Arlene's doubles, her recreations of herself in her own fictional story, apparently as part of her experimentation. The first is Avis M. Watkins, who first miraculously escapes death at eight years old just as Arlene first does (149–50), and later experiences another miraculous escape of death while she is with Arlene (151–52). The physical appearance of Avis with Arlene would seem to indicate that she is "real" and not fictional. However, having the same miraculous experience Arlene had at the same age first suggests that she could be a fictional double recreated by Arlene in Arlene's story. Then, the account of the second miraculous escape when she is with Arlene suggests this recreation even more, because their bodies are close and they seem to become one. As the train that they miraculously avoid approaches, Avis "put one arm around Arlene's shoulder and one hand behind the woman's head and pulled it into the crook of her own neck" (152). Avis's repetition of the voices of characters in Arlene's miraculous escape stories is another indication that she could be part of Arlene's own story: Arlene "had heard [Avis's] voice before, but she had heard it years and years before, and it had belonged to someone [in one of her fictional stories] who was not alive anymore" (153). It is hard to distinguish between the fictional and the real, but all of the "real" and the fictional about Avis's portrayal above is a good possibility in this very experimental story.

Another character whom Arlene could be recreating in her own fictional story is Eulogia Rios, the poor Guatemalan of the title. Eulogia is an artist like Arlene, and she had a miraculous escape from death when she was eight, just like Arlene and Avis, the other fictional recreation of Arlene. When Eulogia was eight years old in school in Guatemala, her teacher was telling the story of her honeymoon on the way to a Peruvian village when soldiers killed the teacher and everyone in Eulogia's school and Guatemalan village except Eulogia, who miraculously survived. At eighteen now, Eulogia paints dead people from her village to recreate their lives in order to finish the teacher's honeymoon story about the Peruvian village she was approaching. The paintings are about people in Guatemala, and the teacher was telling a story about Peru. However, the paintings are a response to the unfinished story: "I never heard the end of her honeymoon story" (157). The point is that artistic/fictional stories, including paintings, connect with other *stories* and perpetuate life. Although she is a painter, Eulogia "dreams" the lives of dead people to tell and complete a *story,* just as Arlene by the end will come to realize that her "dreams" of the lives of dead people in her stories do.

Eulogia's later words could further indicate that she is a fictional recreation of Arlene. She tells both Arlene and Avis that she has been looking for them "from the beginning" (159), and "I could only feel that you were somewhere out in the world looking for me as I was looking for you." Eulogia could literally be a real person looking for Arlene and Avis, but her words could mean that she is the same as Arlene, her recreation who is looking for Arlene because she is the same, and looking for Avis too because she is the same. Just before she leaves Arlene and Avis, she says: "How will they [the people in her paintings] be, if we who were present do not blow life into them and create them?" This is cryptic, but it is possible that her words mean that they were all "present" as one—she, Arlene, and Avis—and must all "blow life into them and create them." (In the context of the *Eucharist, Eulogia* could be part of the body of Arlene that saves lives through artistic creation.)

The ending is an argument for Eulogia being a fictional double created by Arlene, and for the whole argument about Arlene's creation of a separate fictional life. The ending is one long paragraph in which Arlene finishes, "blow[s] life into" in a sense, the honeymoon story about Peru that Eulogia's teacher left unfinished and that Eulogia's paintings leave unfinished. (Eulogia says, "The hard [paintings] are yet to come" [158].) On her own honeymoon to Peru, Arlene finishes Eulogia's story as if she created Eulogia and is the same as she. She again separates the actual life that she earlier talked about in the diary from her fictional life. Her husband, Scott, says "I miss Wesleyan [University]" (161), and Arlene says "I miss Holy Cross." Then "A Poor Guatemalan" focuses on Arlene's dreamlike, imaginary, supernatural fictional story: "The road seemed to be shimmering and shuddering as it turned into a huddle of trees only a child's shout away. . . . She seemed to recognize what she was seeing now. A barely noticeable smile came to the edges of her mouth. The bright road eventually came back again and went on a bit until it dipped swiftly and disappeared once more. . . . She could see the eternal road emerge almost miraculously from the valley, still crooked, still shimmering, still full of humanity, and she turned to her new husband to tell him what the path ahead would be like." At the end, as Arlene looks at her husband after the description of the road, the fictional converges with the actual, but one point being made all along is that the fictional storytelling of Arlene perpetuates "real," daily life.

For a long time in "A Poor Guatemalan," Arlene had resisted the life of the storyteller and the tragic stories that she seemed compelled to tell by pursuing science and getting two doctorates (146), but at the end she fully embraces the role of fiction and storyteller. She apparently realizes that the fictional stories in which others die and she miraculously survives, the stories that she seems compelled to tell, are part of the human story that will "miraculously" work itself out on the "still crooked, still shimmering [road], still full of humanity." It seems that the stories of her life of survival filled with the deaths of others are part of the miraculous that perpetuates "humanity" in the daily life "ahead." Further, it is her job as storyteller to tell stories, no matter what kind of stories the storyteller must tell.

Given the references to Holy Cross, one must consider the relationship of the creative life of Arlene to the creative life of Edward P. Jones, who graduated from Holy Cross in 1972. This is the most difficult and experimental Jones story, and maybe the high level of experimentation makes more sense if one associates Arlene with Jones, experimenting very highly in this story fourteen years after the stories in *Lost in the City* in 1992. (Avis Watkins is the character in this story from the corresponding story in *Lost in the City,* "An Orange Line Train to Ballston," but Avis is nothing like the character in *Lost in the City* and the two stories are not alike either. The connection between the stories is not substantive.)

In "Root Worker," the storyteller comes to the realization of her role and discovers the story that she needs to tell, one greatly influenced by the magical and mysterious but also by the realistic and truthful; telling the story is necessary in order for the storyteller to face her own transgression against another person and its consequences for her family and community, and necessary to knit together black family, community, and tradition. "Root Worker" is somewhat less experimental and somewhat less difficult than "A Poor Guatemalan," but its intricacy, subtlety, ambiguity, and nuance are probably greater and harder to explain.

At the end of the story the main character, Dr. Glynnis Holloway, a medical doctor, tells her story after being converted from scientist to storyteller, but early in "Root Worker" the narrator starts cryptically to reveal that she is a storyteller and the story that she later tells, and to reveal that she has always been subconsciously aware of the story. The narrator is describing St. Elizabeth's Psychiatric Hospital in Washington, D.C.: "a few children, the most innocent, had managed to find their lost minds there, only to lose them again. Morton Holloway, the father of the future doctor, would say to Glynnis, newly twelve, that day on K Street, N.E., 'Child, whas done got into you? You lost your ever lovin mind?'" (169–70). It is not clear what this means at this point because the narrator does not place it in a context to understand it, but at the end it does make sense when Glynnis becomes the storyteller and tells her story. Also, in the back of Glynnis's large, expensive home, where she also practices medicine, there is a "garden [and] . . . lovely winding brick path" (165). This brief description of the garden and path seems inconsequential here, but as the story develops, this scene and similar ones increasingly symbolize the highly magical creative world of a full-blown storyteller, which Glynnis will become.

A lot of "Root Worker" deals with finding the cure for the curse that someone has put on Glynnis's mother, Alberta, which imprisons her in periods of insanity in which she thinks witches are riding her; a root worker or conjure woman in Person County, North Carolina, the home of Morton and Alberta, takes Alberta through a process that enables her to recover the story of her own past that dispels the delusions of witch ridings and thus frees her. The root worker, Dr. Imogene, as people in Person County call her, has many mysterious jars of herbal treatments the contents of which she does not understand: "them labels never done me no good. They got to fallin off them jars after a time, I guess cause they knew I didn't no more care bout em than the man in the moon" (185). One jar has an effect on Alberta that the science-derived medicine from St. Elizabeth's Hospital does not have. Glynnis asks: "Which [jar] sent the witches away from my mother? Which one gave her peace?" Imogene confirms that one did send the witches away: "Dr Imogene reached up to the second shelf and took down a jar third from the end of the row." Although Imogene does not know what is in any of the jars, this one seemingly has magical power.

Imogene's magic is not just in the jars. In front of Imogene's house, there is "a kind of garden on both sides of the pathway to the gate" (174), which is reminiscent of the garden and path behind Glynnis's Washington house, and which connects the two women; there are also a larger garden and a forest behind Imogene's house. Imogene and Alberta walk in the garden and into the forest: "Glynnis could see her mother and Imogene, still arm in arm, come to the end of the garden. If the witches came during the night, she had not heard her mother scream. Beyond the garden, there was a wide field of green grass sprinkled with a few yellow and white flowers. . . . The two entwined their arms again and stepped off to the left where, when the field ended, Glynnis could see the beginning of a kind of forest" (179). There seems to be a magical effect in the garden and forest that is already driving away the witches.

However, while Imogene "dabble[s] in the black arts" (174) and uses the magical power of the jars, garden, and forest to help Alberta, she at the same time is the storyteller/artist who tells and elicits stories to get Alberta to recollect and reconstruct her own story of the past, which helps to restore her to sanity. Imogene asked questions "that Alberta had not had to think about for a long time ('What crops your daddy grow?' 'You look like a fresh butter woman, like me. You ever get that butter straight from them clappers?'), and she did not find it easy to root about the locked attic and come up with the answers. But as the afternoon wore on, she seemed to enjoy answering them, as if they were part of a difficult puzzle she was proud of finally coming to master" (174). Later, Alberta seems to recover even more of her story: "They heard Imogene say something and then Alberta nearly shouted, 'Yes, thas right. I almost forgot that, but that is right" (178). Later again, after recovering more of her story under Imogene's tutelage and dispelling the witches, Alberta gives an account that further indicates her restoration: "she decided it was the perfect time to talk about the first time she and Morton met. It was on a narrow street in Durham and it was morning and there was fog, which lasted the whole day" (192). As Alberta gets better, Imogene causes a magical transformation in Glynnis's spirit and perception, which will lead to her developing magical, healing storytelling ability:

> It was in the third week that she began to suspect that they had fully turned a corner and that they might not have to go back to the old ways. That Monday Glynnis awakened in the late morning and looked down to Dr. Imogene attending the garden in the back. The old woman was doing nothing special, simply going to various plants, bending down and touching them momentarily with her fingers. Caressing a few with the back of her hand. . . . How long a period over the years had her mother gone without the witches riding, how long a time had she gone without doing something no sane person would do? She did not believe it had ever been more than a week. And now they were quickly approaching a month. . . . Dr. Imogene stepped into the other section of the garden, and Glynnis, still not fully awake, thought she saw the plants part to make way. A generous breeze came through and it moved the plants and it moved Dr. Imogene's red dress and it moved the curtain at Glynnis's window and it moved the babyish hairs on her arms. Glynnis raised her hands to her face and cried. (182)

Here Imogene is the artist working in the artistic medium of her garden, a medium that empowers Glynnis magically to evoke healing stories, like the one she has evoked in Alberta. Glynnis walks in the magical forest with Imogene, too. When Glynnis tells Imogene's grandson Jesse that she is truly interested in learning what Imogene does as a root worker, he says that she can learn: "Take her by the hand and walk out to the forest this evening after supper" (195). Although the narrator does not describe the walk, the clear implication is that

Glynnis does walk in the forest with Imogene, and apparently not only gets knowledge from "that stuff in [Imogene's] head" (196), but inspiration from the magical forest as well.

Jesse also earlier walked with Glynnis in the magical forest, which "smelled as it might after a heavy rain, though it had not rained" (191), but a little later he infuses a story he tells Glynnis with a bit of realism that affects her later storytelling, too. Jesse is telling a story about one of Imogene's clients who claims that he wants his sexual potency restored because he "cherishes and treasures the ladies" (194–95). Jesse says that "when you hear a man going on and on about his love for women, he is talking pussy" (195). Jesse "sensed [Glynnis] drifting away from what he was saying and that the only way to bring her back was to use a crude word." He wants her to focus on the realistic and truthful in his story, that the man is only a philanderer who wants sex, in spite of his talk about "treasur[ing] the ladies." The realism Glynnis gets from Jesse's story is different from the magical influence of the forest. Both the magical and the realistic go into making Glynnis the storyteller she becomes.

The story that Glynnis must tell, and eventually does tell, ultimately atones for her own transgression, thus making her whole while knitting together family, community, and black tradition at the same time. After returning to Washington, Glynnis has transformed into a "doctor" who treats her patients "out of small mason jars [and with] plants that were now growing in the backyard on either side of the lovely, winding path" (196). This is the same path the narrator describes at the beginning. Now the path means something more magically creative after the trip to North Carolina. She is now the mature storyteller tutored by Imogene, and linked to her by a similarly magical backyard, instead of the novice that she was at the beginning. Being the mature storyteller, she can invoke the magic of storytelling that she has gotten from Imogene and infuse it with realism, as suggested by Jesse. She uses both the magical and the realistic to create a story when the character Maddie asks her if she "knew just how all the witches and everything started with your mother. Was there such a such somethin that happened on such a such day that you can remember? Did Alberta bother such a such somebody without even knowin it?" (196–97).

With a magic-like ability, Glynnis is able to transport herself back over two decades to when she was ten and reenvision the scene that happened, the scene that the narrator cryptically referred to at the beginning to indicate that all along she subconsciously knew the story; the blunt realism of what she said to a woman on the street is part of the story that goes along with its magical creation. That day when she was ten,[5] standing with Morton as he talked to a woman and, impatiently wanting to move on and spend time alone with him, she said to the woman, Millie: "You so black and fat and ugly, I don't know why my daddy even talkin to you. . . . I wish your black self was dead" (200). This is what caused Morton to ask her if she had lost her mind (170). As Glynnis watches the scene on the street when she was ten in her storytelling mind, she speculates that the terribly hurt woman enlisted a root worker to put a curse on Alberta, causing the witch ridings which began two months later.

Imogene has already expelled the witches, and Glynnis's story at the end heals Glynnis and makes her whole more than it helps Alberta. The idea of Glynnis healing herself with her story seems to relate to three anonymous injunctive statements to a "physician-to-be" throughout the story (166, 171, 185). The statements are cryptic but seem to be ironic in talking to the "patient-to-be" about healing. The first statement is perhaps the clearest and indicates the broad meaning of all three: "*Physician-to-be, never heal thyself. Not one soul in this room will ever, no matter what skills you acquire and master here, be able to cure fully the mechanisms of your own machine*" (166). The ironic point could be that Glynnis the physician can heal herself, her "own machine," with her story, which she does.

Besides healing Glynnis herself and solving the mystery of what happened to Alberta, Glynnis's story ties together black traditions. According to the story, perhaps a "root worker strolling by" on the street in Washington (200) heard what she said and had "seen Millie's pain and was determined to set the world straight" (201), which she did by putting the witch-riding curse on Alberta. The root worker on the street in Washington is a fictional figure linking the tradition of the South to that of the North, indicating a sustaining black connection.

"Root Worker" further depicts the linking of black traditions in the South and the North as it complements and completes "The Sunday Following Mother's Day," *Lost in the City*'s corresponding story. Also a character in "The Sunday Following Mother's Day," Maddie has a past history in Person County, North Carolina, and travels back to Person County and then back to Washington, thus creating a back-and-forth sustaining movement grounded in black tradition. Moreover, in "The Sunday Following Mother's Day," Maddie and the other characters cannot tell a story based in southern tradition that sustains and supports by making sense of the apparent curse on her brother, which is like the one someone put on Alberta that made him kill his wife in the middle of the night. In "Root Worker," Washington-born Glynnis (174, 177) travels back to immerse herself in black tradition in North Carolina and then back to Washington, and then tells the connecting black story.

Although "Root Worker" is not as hard to understand as "A Poor Guatemalan," it is still very intricate, subtle, ambiguous, and nuanced. This is true from the beginning, when Glynnis is still a medical doctor but also, unknown to her, the novice storyteller linked to Imogene by similar magical backyards (165, 178), and the novice storyteller because of the apparent incipient appearance of the story in her subconscious (169–70); to the portrayal of all the richly ambiguous interaction of Glynnis with Imogene, Jesse, and other characters that make Glynnis a mature storyteller; to the characterization of Imogene as storyteller/artist who gets Alberta to tell her story and influences Glynnis as a storyteller; to all the story's cryptic passages; to the end where Glynnis, now a "doctor"/storyteller who treats her patients "out of small mason jars" (196) with the help of plants growing in her magical backyard beside the path, tells her story of a root worker in Washington. The long, convoluted preceding sentence is meant to reflect the intricacy, subtlety, ambiguity, and nuance of this story about the artist and artistry, the longest story in either of these volumes.

A primary theme of "Tapestry" is the development of the tapestry maker to her maturity as a creative artist; further, the narrator constructs several manqué narratives that lead to one final, conclusive narrative in a process of telling a story, thus symbolizing the way an artist creates by choosing among and revising various plots. "Tapestry" is the last story in *All Aunt Hagar's Children* and the one that is most forthrightly about the creative artist and artistry, therefore making the dominant thematic direction of the volume clear at the end.

The Picayune, Mississippi, home of the tapestry maker Anne Perry symbolizes her immaturity as an artist at the beginning, but during the course of the story she develops from the picayunish artist to the mature one. Instead of choosing crochet, as her sister does, Anne chooses the artistic medium of tapestry, which in the words of her grandmother is "somethin that will stay round for a hundred years. Maybe even a thousand" (377). The grandmother is correct in seeing the long-lasting artistic value of tapestry, and so Anne's choice of this form is an important statement about her potential from the beginning. However, Anne also goes through an artistic development as shown in her later revision in Washington, D.C., of a tapestry that she began in Picayune. After her father sent the old tapestry from Mississippi to her in Washington six years later, "She would have by then grown into something else in Washington and had barely enough left of Mississippi in her to finish the snow scene [she had started]. It took three more years, but it looked nothing like the world she had first imagined in Picayune" (389). Now an artist with a more mature imagination, Anne is involved in an ongoing creative process that takes years.

The overall story told by the narrator shows a creative process implying that the narrator is a creator doing much of the same thing that Anne is doing. The narrator presents several narratives of Anne's life that would have happened if she had married men in Picayune instead of George Carter from Washington (375–79). In one narrative, when Anne would have died after her husband, the preacher at her funeral would have said: "We're jealous of God this mornin' . . . cause He's sittin with our Anne and we won't be able to sit and talk with her again until nine and a half minutes after we step through them Pearly Gates" (378–79). Since none of this actually happens, though, these narratives only allude to a process of creation and revision of Anne's story. After Anne's decision to break up with her new husband, George, on the train on her way to Washington from Picayune, the narrator presents several other narratives describing her return to Picayune (393–97); the narratives end, "Then she would be home" (397). However, again, none of what happens in the narratives actually occurs, and the narratives allude to the narrator's creation and revision of Anne's story. The narrator describes the train: "Thin smoke wafted through her train" (394); "the lights of her train dimmed" (396); "her train began an awful shaking" (397). These descriptions are devices the narrator uses to set up the presentation of the manqué narratives that indicate the creative, revisionary process. Later, the narrator says "the entire train seemed to stop its shaking and rattling" (399), which signals that the manqué narratives are almost over and the story is close to the final version of Anne's narrative. In this final version, Anne will be a resident of Washington. After the "train slowed," Anne comes to terms with her Washington reality: "Mama, I'm a long way from home." The story ends: "Papa, I'm a long way from home."

Anne will be a resident of Washington who carries with her the black history and tradition of Mississippi and the South, which is the collective history and tradition of the people on the train. The stories of her sleeping husband George and the other black people asleep on the train symbolize this history and tradition. George says: "*I'll do it. . . . I'll clean every barn before I sleep, master. No need for that thing. No need for that again. I'll do it. I told yall I'd do it all*" (398). "The sounds of the other sleepers now came to her as well, and there were many who were also talking in their sleep. Men and women speaking whole thoughts. A shout or two. A plea." However, the strength to survive the legacy of this same oppressive history and tradition, which the sleepers' lives imply, will be a part of what sustains them as they move from the South to the North, as is always true in Jones's stories.

Finally, "Tapestry" complements "Marie," the corresponding story in *Lost in the City,* by expanding its ideas about black creativity. The character Marie is the subconscious carrier of black stories and traditions that she surprisingly reproduces on tape recordings, but Anne in "Tapestry" goes beyond Marie because Anne is the conscious artist who goes through a process of maturing as artist in the story. Also, the common character in both stories is George Carter, the grandson of Anne and George Carter in "Tapestry." He is not born at the time of "Tapestry," but the narrator looks ahead and mentions that he later does tape recordings of the stories of his grandmother and grandfather, just as he does tape recordings of Marie. Typical of Jones's writing, the stories flow back and forth over time and generations.

CHAPTER 6

Jones's Vision and Its Development

In his novel, *The Known World,* and volumes of short stories, *Lost in the City* and *All Aunt Hagar's Children,* perhaps the most stunning thing about Edward P. Jones's writing is its spectacular vision that encompasses everything, a historical whole, a totality of African American experience. From the perspective of a godlike omniscient narrator in the novel, and a similar third-person omniscient perspective in most of the stories, this vision sees African American life in distinct time periods, but also simultaneously in the future, the past, and the present. Especially but not exclusively in the novel, this vision, that can be up close to the pain and tragedy of oppression but also can move a distance from it at any particular instance, creates a perspective that is structurally fragmented but memorably incisive. The distance of this perspective makes it possible for the narrator to speak about oppression in a wry, humorous voice and to take an unconventional ironic approach.

This totality of vision stretches from an indefinite time in American slavery to the present, and it reveals a range of socioeconomic classes of black people and Americans in general over this period. Black people make social and economic progress, but the main emphasis is not the progress from the nineteenth century forward. Instead, the totality of vision emphasizes a stasis of time as much as discrete times, and if anything black slaves and ex-slaves in the novel, who were more overtly, severely oppressed, played more salient roles in fighting oppression. In this context, the key for freed black people is to maintain a connection with their legacy of struggle through the tradition that slaves established; slaves and former slaves in the novel are in closer proximity to and maintain this traditional connection better than the characters in the short-story collections, who primarily live free lives and are ironically much more "lost." The characters in the short stories must find or reconnect with the tradition that the slaves in *The Known World* could not very well forget. Also, the end of *The Known World* and several stories in *All Aunt Hagar's Children* focus on the artist and artistry, and foreground the importance of the artist and art in portraying the vision of the totality of the African American experience that implies the importance of connection to tradition. This suggests the role that Jones himself must take as a writer in maintaining the legacy of struggle.

Throughout Jones's work, his vision projects faith and hope in African Americans and their traditional struggle against oppression. Ultimately the vision is a moral one that emphasizes right and justice for black people in the fight against white oppression; further, usually oriented in favor of "grassroots" black people in the South and Washington, D.C., the vision emphasizes positive, progressive, moral action in the black community that will build on the tradition of the past. The morality in this vision is a major component of Jones's work that should not be forgotten. Maybe this strong feeling about what is right comes from Jones's connection to his mother, who struggled so hard in a world that put strong obstacles in her way and from his own sense of personal struggle, but it is significant in his work, no matter its origin.

Jones largely developed his vision over the years from the 1980s, when he published uncollected short stories, to 1992, when he published *Lost in the City,* to 2003, when he published *The Known World*. One can explain his vision's development by looking at what Jones has said in an interview about his writing in the 1980s and examining the uncollected published stories from the 1980s.

Writing was secondary in Jones's life in the 1980s: "For a long time writing wasn't really all that important to me, not as much as it should have been. I was never one to get up every day and do it. From '83 on until '88, '89, I would just do it every now and again. Then on this day job that I had, there were two guys there who died, and they had wanted to be writers. I think that I felt rather guilty about the fact that a lot of people had said that I could write and I wasn't doing it, and these guys who wanted to do it were no longer around. So I started working on *Lost in the City*" (Golden 56–57).

Even after the publication of *Lost in the City,* Jones's personal struggles continued to shape his vision in *The Known World*. As he put it:

> I lived in this apartment in Arlington from '83 until 2004, twenty-one years. After *Lost in the City* came out, I had been thinking up this thing that became a novel, *The Known World*. But I hadn't really sat down and done any writing. In '99, these new people bought the apartment building, and they didn't make the people above me on the tenth floor put down

> carpeting and they were loud and noisy and that really had an effect on me. I had already suffered a bout of depression and been on and off medicine.
>
> It was one of the worst times ever in my life. There are about four or five things I can point to in life along this line, and the first one is the death of my mother, and this four-and-a-half-year period from '99 to 2004 with these people above me was another. I suffered through all of that, and at times I would take this medicine. For all these years, the book *The Known World* was gelling in my head. Then I lost the day job that I had for nineteen years. I wondered how was I going to get a job? But rather than saying, you have no job, what are you going to do now, I had a plan for the novel because I had been working on it for ten years in my head. And the writing of it said you can put aside the misery for now. . . . These people that were in the novel, they carried me through. And over time, as more and more of the book came out on the computer, the pain of it all banished. I was writing the book based on all the books I have ever read, knowing what was good and what was not good. Knowing that you can't be stereotypical, that every character you come up with, whether Black or White, has to be given his or her due. Even the worst criminal in the novel, there was a moment when this person was a good person perhaps, whether it was when they were one or two years old. Your job with the worst person in the novel is to find out when that day was. When you write, you want to go down a road that no other writer has gone down. (57–58)

Jones's comments suggest the seriousness, depth, and power of his vision that really started to develop in the 1980s. The unpublished stories from the 1980s that he alludes to in the interview provide points of comparison showing the difference between Jones's incipient vision of that time and his later mature vision.

"The Farmer's Palace" (*Callaloo* 1981) is primarily about Hezekiah Battle, who is living in a small town in Virginia with his wife, Miriam, and is mourning the death of his aunt in Philadelphia. He blames himself because he never took his aunt's side or stood up for her when his father (her brother) called her a whore and greatly chastised her because she, "at that age where [Hezekiah and his father] thought no man would be interested in her" (6), decided to marry and move to Philadelphia with her husband. Hezekiah also feels that he was disloyal and virtually deserted his aunt, leaving her to live alone in Philadelphia after her husband's death. In spite of what he sees as the grave mistreatment of his aunt, she leaves Hezekiah a large inheritance from the property of her storeowner husband when she dies, which he uses to open a store that he names the Farmer's Palace. Another character in the story is also mourning and suffering.

Robert Adams, the husband of Hezekiah's godchild, blames himself for not getting his wife and children out of a burning house before they died. Also, two sisters in the story, one a prostitute and the other a mother angry with her sister for exposing her children to an illicit life, are causing controversy in the town because of the rift in their relationship. Near the end, Hezekiah listens in the night to the prostitute laughing wildly with a man as Hezekiah observes the drunk, sad Robert who is asleep. Then, "he found that he wanted to say something to the sleeping man, perhaps the same words he wanted someone now to say to him" (13). He "was suddenly aware of an emotional exhaustion, like that of someone who had been crying all day."

The tone of "The Farmer's Palace" is forlorn, and it seems to show that two of its characters cannot get over tragedy and heartache. This is not unusual or remarkable in Jones's fiction or anyone else's, but at the same time the contour of the characters, plot, and theme pale in comparison to Jones's stories in his later volumes. After Hezekiah returned from visiting his aunt in Philadelphia once, he did have nightmares about "being lost in the city," which of course invokes the title of the later volume of stories with all of its power, but this story does not have that power. The trip from Virginia to Philadelphia and back does not present the potential of sustaining connection between the South and the North that makes the later stories so provocative.

Hortense Stuart in "Island" (*Ploughshares* 1983) is a woman who has to come to terms with the consequences of her past, in which she became pregnant by a man named Lucas from a town nearby, South Boston, Virginia. Lucas is now living in New York, but over eleven years ago he impregnated Hortense while he was home visiting and, although it is not completely clear, apparently promised to send her a ticket to come to be with him in New York (65). The ticket never came, and as the time for the birth of her child neared, Hortense, a woman ignorant of the rudiments of geography, tried to walk to New York to find Lucas before the child was born (65). Tired and worn out, she managed to find her way to the cabin of Absalom Stuart on a so-called "island" close-by. Absalom helped deliver her child, a girl, and let her stay with him, eventually marrying her and having a second child, a boy, by her. In the present, in town from the island to get medicine for her sick son, Hortense encounters Lucas, home to visit his dying mother. Lucas recognizes Hortense but refuses to acknowledge her. This brings back a deluge of pain about the past, but also forces Hortense to consider that she still loves the reprobate Lucas instead of Stuart, who has done so much for her and whom she had convinced herself she now loves. On the way to town, Hortense had seen and visited the cabin of an old woman, Miss Sally, who told Hortense the story of her estrangement from her children. Miss Sally says, "But why would God let my chirren leave me floatin out here like this?" (66). At the end, Hortense conflates her pain and confusion about her feelings for Absalom and Lucas after eleven years with Miss Sally's: "If not eleven years, then . . . ? *They shouldna left me floatin out here, hon*" (71).

As in "The Farmer's Palace," heartache and pain dominate. Again, however, nothing stands out about the story in the way that Jones's stories in the volumes are so often outstanding. The reader has no sense of going "down a road that no other writer has gone down," which Jones says is his goal in writing *The Known World,* and which many readers think he accomplishes in both the novel and many of the short stories. The other uncollected story, "Harvest" (*Essence* 1976), is also about a woman who gets pregnant when young and unmarried. The story reveals more years of her life than "Island" reveals of Hortense's, but the pregnancy negatively shapes her entire life in a way similar to that in which the pregnancy shapes Hortense's. An unremarkable gloom pervades the story much as it does the other two early stories.

The stunning, spectacular vision in the later short-story volumes and the novel is not clearly enough defined and articulated in the uncollected stories to give events force and effect, to raise characters in high relief above the mundane and insipid, and generally to lift the stories above a flat monotone to the level of the outstanding and memorable. Part of the reason is that in the uncollected stories the pathway back and forth between the South and the North, the sustaining connection, is only an idea in its incipient stages. This connection strongly informs the vision of a totality that makes Jones's fiction original, unique, and powerful. Without this connection, the early stories and their characters do not have the same verve and freshness. The stories are plaintive but not outstanding or memorable.

This comparison between the early writing and the later stories and novel is not put forth to criticize Edward P. Jones, but to emphasize how far he has come since he decided to be serious as a writer. The vision of black experience he has developed that encompasses Washington, D.C.; Virginia; and many southern states, and that moves over distinct times and simultaneously unites all time, is one of the most remarkable in literature. His vision makes Jones one of the most compelling writers in contemporary fiction and makes it possible to compare him to literary greats such as William Faulkner, Richard Wright, and James Joyce who have developed similarly remarkable visions of time and place. He has already won the Pulitzer Prize and the PEN/Hemingway Award and has been nominated for the National Book Award. One hopes that, with his vast talent, Jones will write additional fictional works and continue to be a powerful force that further enriches American literature and the literary world.

NOTES

Chapter 2: Meaning, Structure, and Story in *The Known World*

1. In a section appended to the Amistad edition of *The Known World* (4) and in an interview (Iris Nicole Johnson 89), Jones has referred to his role as the god of his characters.

2. Sarah Mutter suggests that the large number of characters might symbolize slavery's creation of "'thingly' humans [who] may be accounted for impersonally, mathematically" (127). The large number of characters shows slavery treating people like inanimate objects that can be represented by mathematical calculations.

3. We can think of all of the episodes as mini-stories. Susan V. Donaldson states that the "multiple stories that crowd the pages of Jones's novel suggest something of the approaching demise of [slavery's] mastery" (273) because the mini-stories are challenging its *one* large, dominant story, the story that black people are inferior and therefore that slavery is right.

4. The omniscient narrator has a godlike vision related to the novel and its characters that is essentially that of Edward P. Jones, the author, but this vision is not the same as the vision and power of God in whom the characters have faith.

5. Chelsea Wiksyk characterizes the relationship between Robbins and Philomena as lacking mutual respect, but his "relationship with their children is more deeply grounded in mutual love and respect" (64).

6. Mutter says "Henry Townsend has been enslaved, and *could be* enslaved; he just happens, in the moment of the novel, not to be. That he nonetheless chooses to actively participate in a chattel system as a slaveowner is strange, and deeply ironic" (135).

7. Katherine Clay Bassard shows that both Calvin's photograph of the "frozen dog" and Alice's artwork at the end of the novel represent imaginary worlds that oppose the novel's known world (417–18).

8. There are "two characters who retain their sense of self-worth despite repeated attacks on their autonomy: Augustus and Jebediah" (Wiksyk 70). Although he is a slave, Jebediah's respect for himself as a human being is what will eventually teach Fern something about human equality.

9. The omniscient narrator describes Augustus, after he dies, as rising up above everything and then walking back to Mildred in Virginia: "Augustus's spirit is already striding home to Mildred, a final reminder of the part of Augustus that could not be restrained" (Wiksyk 71).

10. "Insurance policies on material properties consistently cover the complete destruction or 'death' of that property. Jones's choice to elucidate the many ways a slave could die [*The Known World* 355–56] and then have [the insurance agent] carefully

refuse to insure each one points clearly at the difference between material property and a slave" (Wiksyk 69). It is also ironic that insurance policies on "material properties" give larger coverage than policies on human beings.

11. Susan V. Donaldson describes the symbolism of freedom in Alice's art: "Alice's wondrous creations testify to the central truths denied by slavery and by American racism: not the rigid separation of master and slave, and white and black, but the close intertwining of the two" (281). Laura Dawkins sees in Alice's artwork a symbol of her own physical escape to freedom: "Alice's artistic achievements attest to her continued subversion of the master's 'known world' even after her escape from slavery" (129). Dawkins also says that Alice's art stands in opposition to the map of the "known world" in John Skiffington's office (*The Known World* 174–75). She further connects Alice's vision to the omniscient narrator's: "the 'God's-eye view' of Alice's work of art replicates the omniscient narrative voice of *The Known World,* which moves easily among past, present, and future perspectives" (133).

12. Mutter describes Celeste and Elias's freedom in terms reminiscent of Calvin's imaginary free world: "Both Elias and Celeste realize, and embrace, the possibility of an alternate universe, a 'whole world' distinct from—and contradictory to—the one they otherwise occupy. As Elias carves—a comb for his wife, a doll for his daughter, a horse for his son—he carves a 'whole world' for himself and his family, a world that allows them all to 'get over'—by somehow getting out of—their actual world, 'the world of human property'" (142). Mutter indicates that Alice's art serves a similar purpose to Elias's (143–44).

Chapter 3: *The Known World*'s Characters

1. In interviews, Jones always talks about his great love and respect for his mother. For example, he says that "ninety percent of what I remember and use in [*All Aunt Hagar's Children* (2006)] has to do with my mother" (Graham 432).

2. Jones's illiterate mother, Jeanette, kept him and his two siblings together with her after Jones's father left before he started school. Jeanette "struggled to keep them together by working multiple jobs as a maid and dishwasher. They moved 18 times in 18 years. 'Each place was worse than the last,' recalls Jones" (Murphy 23).

3. More critics write about Alice than Celeste. They note Alice's obvious feigned madness and trickery, but the biggest topic is her artwork that the novel depicts at the end. See Laura Dawkins (129–34), Iris Nicole Johnson (148–50), and Jonathan Howard (17–25), for example.

4. Carolyn Berman interprets this passage as part of the novel's "re-membering of lost time" (236).

5. David Ikard says that the novel's "most profound engagement with white supremacist ideology, slavery, and African American consciousness involves slave owner Fern Elston and runaway slave Jebediah Dickson" (81). Iris Nicole Johnson talks about Fern's family-like relationship with her slaves, and then the empathy that she develops for Dickson: "The emotion, sorrow she feels toward the crippled slave moves her to set him free. His anguish forces her to see him as more than property, or even family" (139–40).

6. Besides showing her superficiality and selfishness, Caldonia's relationship with Moses reveals "ways white supremacist models of domination bankrupt the moral claims and critical insights of the African American elite" (Ikard 79–81). Other critics also talk about Caldonia's relationship with Henry. Katherine Bassard says: "Perhaps the

most disturbing aspect of Caldonia's character is the way in which she uses her power as slaveholder for the purposes of sexual exploitation of a black male slave" (413). Iris Nicole Johnson analyzes the relationship between Caldonia and Moses, and also analyzes the dynamics of Caldonia's family, a family in which her mother, Maude, sees slave ownership as a legacy and her brother, Calvin, opposes slavery (141–48). Further, see Dawkins's critique of Caldonia's acceptance of the ideology of slavery (125–28). Dawkins discusses her relationship with Moses, and briefly discusses her opposition to her brother and her similarity to her mother.

7. Ikard says that Clara's "schizophrenic behavior toward Ralph [is] an emotional manifestation of her ideological investment in white supremacy" (68–69). He also says that the fact that Ralph stays after slavery is over shows that he "has an ideological and emotional stake in this parasitical relationship" (71).

8. Wiksyk says that "Augustus's spirit . . . already striding home to Mildred [is] a final reminder of the part of Augustus that could not be restrained" (71).

9. Sarah Mahurin Mutter talks about the importance of love and family to Elias, who ". . . is buoyed by love [of Celeste]." Also, when he "refigures himself as belonging to a nuclear family, he gains a measure of subjectivity as well as a more palatable, more humanized understanding of 'belonging'" (129).

10. Iris Nicole Johnson discusses Augustus's skilled artistry as a means to free his family from slavery (137–39). She makes a statement about Augustus that relates to the point about the irony of his being a skilled artist with the wherewithal to purchase freedom, but whose family line nevertheless ends in slavery: Augustus "dies a slave, leaving behind no evidence of his skilled artistry" (138).

11. Bassard quotes the passage referring to Calvin's photograph with the dog looking to the right at a whole different world, and states that Calvin's "sexuality and anti-slavery views" mark him as one of the "disrupters of 'the known world'" (417).

12. Several critics analyze Robbins's indoctrination of Henry and the failure of his own father to influence him. See Bassard (412–13, 416–17), Iris Nicole Johnson (134–39), Dawkins (120–25), and Wiksyk (66–68).

13. See Ikard for a discussion of Barnum's struggle over morality and racism (71–73).

14. Making a point different from the one made here, Jonathan Howard talks about Skiffington's inability to remember Mildred and Augustus's names because of his racism and the racist society around him (15–18).

15. Ikard talks about Robbins being his own "worst enemy" (74) because his investment in the ideology of slavery confuses him about his feelings for Philomena (74–76). Wiksyk also provides some insights about Robbins' relationship with Philomena and his children by her (63–64).

Chapter 4: The Stories of *Lost in the City*

1. From the short interview in "About the Author," a section at the end of the Harper Collins Amistad edition of *The Known World*, 2004.

2. General tradition means the life and historical reality of the majority of black people that is grounded in the South, as opposed to a more specific practice, belief, or way of doing things among black people in different places at different times. The idea of oppression is encompassed in the concept of general tradition, but so are overcoming oppression and surviving as a race through strength and determination.

3. Although Jessica Maucione is not speaking as broadly and not saying the same thing, what she says basically supports the point being made here: "Jones suggests . . .

that one way of coping with the forms of dehumanization particular to the . . . North is to draw upon cultural values associated with the rural South. . . . The attempt to import these values into Washington's black neighborhoods sometimes lead to heartbreak, but the effort also infuses the neighborhoods with a sense of home that makes survival possible—and sometimes, too, a quality of life beyond survival" (81).

4. The subconscious is memories that are hidden from the conscious awareness of characters but that motivating circumstances and situations can bring to conscious awareness.

5. Along with the portrayal of the plight of Washington, D.C., black communities in *Lost in the City,* Jones also portrays black communities, somewhat paradoxically but very strikingly, as places of safety, which goes along with the idea of the importance of supportive black community in this volume and in *All Aunt Hagar's Children.* Jessica M. Brown talks about "safe spaces" in Washington in the stories in *Lost in the City* (12–19), "The Girl Who Raised Pigeons" among them. Brown says: "In the absence of a mother, Betsy Ann is effectively raised by the Myrtle Street inhabitants. She is provided for by the teacher who lives next door, the doctor who lives down the street and a land lady who serves as a surrogate grandmother" (17). So, although the white community has encroached on the black community at the end, this example of community is there for Betsy Ann to carry on. All the stories do not end like "The Girl," but the idea that black communities are "safe spaces," although sometimes consumed by the white menace around them, is there in several stories. Maucione also makes a comment about community in *Lost in the City* that coincides with the above: "While Jones's characters are at various measures of remove from the South and slavery and are variously displaced and displacing, *Lost in the City* serves as a textual resurrection of the neighborhood that, however fleetingly, did once provide a sense of belonging and sanctuary" (77). This "textual resurrection" is what one sees in "The Girl Who Raised Pigeons," which Maucione talks about in the next paragraph.

6. It is ironic that, as one critic notes, the well-educated Lydia might be the "most lost" among all the characters in *Lost in the City* (McCarron 11–12). Two other critics also imply that Lydia's situation may be the worst: "The idea of lostness receives its most complex treatment . . . in the collection's title story, in which Jones depicts the dilemma of Lydia Walsh, an affluent graduate of Yale Law School who lives among white people and owns a posh town house" (Kennedy and Beuka 13).

7. The unconscious is that part of the mind that cannot be known by the conscious part. This is a shortened and simplified version of Sigmund Freud's definition.

8. This story is autobiographical, to an extent. The mother takes the girl to another school where the authorities do not allow her to enroll before she goes to a second school. Jones has said: "My mother and I, as in the story 'The First day,' did go to [another] school and were told I was supposed to be someplace else. After that . . . I don't remember anything. So everything about this [mother]. . . is out of my imagination, because I don't recall what actually happened. I do remember we set off that day and were told we had to go someplace else" (Elam 127–28). When asked who has influenced him besides his mother, he makes the importance of his mother clear: "What my mother taught me was enough; I don't need to learn from anyone else" (128). So the fact that he cannot remember beyond a point what happened on the first day his mother took him to school does not at all diminish her importance to him.

Chapter 5: The Stories of *All Aunt Hagar's Children*

1. General tradition means the life and historical reality of the majority of black people that is grounded in the South, as opposed to a more specific practice, belief, or way of doing things among black people in different places at different times. The idea of oppression is encompassed in the concept of general tradition, but so is overcoming oppression and surviving as a race through strength and determination. The omniscient narrator in "In the Blink of God's Eye," the first story in *All Aunt Hagar's Children,* describes two characters in a way that places them in a context of historical oppression, struggle, and survival of oppression synonymous with general tradition: "They were the children of once-upon-a-time slaves, born into a kind of freedom, but they had traveled down through the wombs with what all their kind had been born with—the knowledge that God had promised next week to everyone but themselves" (10).

2. The subconscious is the reality hidden from the conscious awareness of characters, but that motivating circumstances and situations can bring to conscious awareness.

3. Postmodernism encompasses a wide range of creative and critical practices. One practice in creative writing is placing in the foreground or making explicit the role of creativity and the creative artist in fiction, as in Jones's stories in this volume.

4. The idea of triumph in the theme of "All Aunt Hagar's Children" relates to the biblical Hagar in Genesis, who was oppressed but gave birth to a child who fathered a nation (Genesis 21: 9–13). Regarding the volume's title and this story's title, Jones has said: "I didn't necessarily think about the biblical reference. The phrase 'All Aunt Hagar's Children' was a phrase my mother used for black people, and that was it. That was all I meant. Richard Wright wrote a collection of stories called *Uncle Tom's Children*, and I had been impressed when I read that in my teens. So, I think I just wanted to give a nod to him as well with the title" (Elam 132–33). Aunt Penny in "All Aunt Hagar's Children" says: "'It's a shame before God, the way they do all Aunt Hagar's children'" (106). A character in "Common Law" in *All Aunt Hagar's Children* also uses the phrase in reference to burying her abusive husband, whom she killed: "she thought all Aunt Hagar's children deserved a place in the ground" (223).

5. On page 170, the narrator says Glynnis was twelve; on page 198, the narrator says she was ten.

BIBLIOGRAPHY

Primary Works

NOVEL

The Known World. 2003. New York: HarperCollins, 2004.

SHORT STORY COLLECTIONS

All Aunt Hagar's Children. 2006. New York: HarperCollins, 2007.
Lost in the City. 1992. New York: HarperCollins, 1993.

UNCOLLECTED STORIES

"The Farmer's Palace." *Callaloo* 11–13 (February–October 1981): 1–13.
"Harvest." *Essence* 7.7 (November 1976): 84, 108–10, 112, 114–15, 128.
"Island." *Ploughshares* 9.2–3 (1983): 53–71.

Secondary Works

Bassard, Katherine Clay. "Imagining Other Worlds: Race, Gender, and the 'Power Line' in Edward P. Jones's *The Known World*." *African American Review* 42.3–4 (Fall–Winter 2008): 407–19.

Berman, Carolyn Vellenga. "*The Known World* in World Literature: Bakhtin, Glissant, and Edward P. Jones." *Novel: A Forum on Fiction* 42.2 (Summer 2009): 231–38.

Brown, Jessica M. "Narrating Washington, D.C. from the Margins: Urban Space and Cultural Identity in *Lost in the City* and *The Beautiful Things That Heaven Bears*." *Berkeley Undergraduate Journal* 23.2 (2011): 1–35. escholarship.org/uc/item/9kw5m22b.

Dawkins, Laura. "Inside and Outside the Master's House: The Architecture of Power in *The Known World*." In *Edward P. Jones: New Essays*, ed. Wood, 117–34.

Donaldson, Susan V. "Telling Forgotten Stories of Slavery in the Postmodern South." *Southern Literary Journal* 40.2 (Spring 2008): 267–83.

Donica, Joseph L. V. "Hierarchies of Knowledge and the Limits of Law and Theology in *The Known World*." In *Edward P. Jones: New Essays*, ed. Wood, 135–57.

"Edward P. Jones." *Encyclopedia of World Biography*. www.notablebiographies.com/newsmakers2/2005-Fo-La/Jones-Edward-P.html.

Elam, Angela. "To Make a Story: An Interview with Edward P. Jones." *New Letters* 74.1 (2007): 121–35.

Golden, Marita, ed. "Edward P. Jones." In *The Word: Black Writers Talk About the Transformative Power of Reading and Writing,* 47–60. New York: Random House, 2011.

Gonzalez, Christopher. "Spatialization and Deictic Shifts in *Lost in the City* and *All Aunt Hagar's Children.*" In *Edward P. Jones: New Essays,* ed. Wood, 185–202.

Graham, Maryemma. "An Interview with Edward P. Jones." *African American Review* 42.3–4 (Fall–Winter 2008): 421–38.

Harris, Trudier. "The Worst Fear Imaginable: Black Slave Owners in Edward P. Jones's *The Known World.*" *The Scary Mason-Dixon Line: African American Writers and the South.* Baton Rouge: Louisiana State University Press, 2009. 174–94.

Henry, Lorraine M. "Mr. Jones's Neighborhoods: The Triad of Place, History, and Memory in *Lost in the City* and *All Aunt Hagar's Children.*" In *Edward P. Jones: New Essays,* ed. Wood, 161–84.

Howard, Jonathan. "Their Eyes Were God's: A Counter-Cartography of *The Known World.*" *2009–2010 Penn Humanities Forum on Connections.* epository.upenn.edu/uhf_2010/10/.

Ikard, David. "White Supremacy under Fire: The Unrewarded Perspective in Edward P. Jones's *The Known World.*" *Melus* 36.3 (Fall 2011): 63–85.

Jackson, Tommie. "Slave Patrols in *The Known World.*" *CLA Journal* 53.2 (December 2009): 162–77.

Johnson, Iris Nicole. "Contemporary Ownership: The Master, the Slave, and the Self in Edward P. Jones's *The Known World.*" *Revisiting Slave Narratives II: Les avatars contemporains des recruits d'sclaves II.* Collected by Judith Misrahi-Barak. Montpellier, France: Presses universitaires de la Méditerranée, 2007. 129–54.

Johnson, Sarah Anne. "The Image You Woke Up With." *The Very Telling: Conversations with American Writers.* Lebanon, N.H.: University Press of New England, 2006. 82–91.

Kennedy, J. Gerald, and Robert Beuka. "Imperiled Communities in Edward P. Jones's *Lost in the City* and Dagoberto Gilb's *The Magic of Blood.*" *Yearbook of English Studies* 31 (2001): 10–23.

MacKenzie, Cameron. "The City of Being: Space, Trauma, and Identity in *Lost in the City.*" In *Edward P. Jones: New Essays,* ed. Wood, 93–114.

Marshall, Stephen. "Taking Liberty Behind God's Back: Mastery as the Central Problem of Slavery." *Polity* 44 (2012): 155–81.

Maucione, Jessica. "Neighborhood as the New Lost World in *Lost in the City.*" In *Edward P. Jones: New Essays,* ed. Wood, 75–91.

McCarron, Bill. "Most Lost in Edward P. Jones's *Lost in the City.*" *Notes on Contemporary Literature* 36.2 (March 2006): 11–12.

Murphy, Michelle P. "Edward P. Jones '72 & *The Known World.*" *Holy Cross Magazine* 38.3 (Summer 2004): 23–27.

Mutter, Sarah Mahurin. "'Such a Poor Word for a Wondrous Thing': Thingness and the Recovery of the Human in *The Known World.*" *Southern Literary Journal* 43.2 (Spring 2011): 125–46.

Pinkmountain, Scott. "It Gets You Through: The Rumpus Interview with Edward P. Jones." *The Rumpus* (May 2, 2011). therumpus.net/2011/05/it-gets-you-through-the-rumpus-interview-with-edward-p-jones/.

Pressly, Thomas J. "*The Known World* of Free Black Slaveholders: A Research Note on the Scholarship of Carter G. Woodson." *Journal of African American History* 91.1 (Winter 2006): 81–87.

Saunders, James Robert. "A World of Irony in the Fiction of Edward P. Jones." *Hollins Critic* 44.1 (February 2007): 1–10.

Torday, Daniel. "Young Boys and Old Lions: Fatalism in the Stories of Edward P. Jones." *Literary Imagination* 11.3 (2009): 349–65.

Wiksyk, Chelsea. "Navigating and Negating the Ownership Fallacy in Edward P. Jones's *The Known World*." *Albatross* 2.1 (2012): 59–72.

Wood, Daniel Davis. "Anatomizing a Body of Work: A Survey of Critical Analyses of the Jones *Oeuvre*." In *Edward P. Jones: New Essays*, ed. Wood, 61–71.

———. "Beyond City Limits: Edward P. Jones's Uncollected Short Fiction." In *Edward P. Jones: New Essays*, ed. Wood, 205–11.

———, ed. *Edward P. Jones: New Essays*. Melbourne, Australia: Whetstone Press, 2011.

———. "Reader, Writer, Mentor, Man: A Portrait of Edward P. Jones." In *Edward P. Jones: New Essays*, ed. Wood, 11–59.

INDEX